Disputed Questions on Virtue

Disputed Questions on Virtue

Quaestio Disputata de Virtutibus In Communi and *Quaestio Disputata de Virtutibus Cardinalibus*

Thomas Aquinas

Translation and Preface by Ralph McInerny

ST. AUGUSTINE'S PRESS
South Bend, Indiana

Manufactured in the United States of America.

1 2 3 4 5 6   15 14 13 12 11 10 09

Library of Congress Cataloging in Publication Data
Thomas, Aquinas, Saint, 1225?-1274.
  [Quaestio disputata de virtutibus in communi. English]
  Disputed questions on virtue / Thomas Aquinas : translated with a preface by Ralph McInerny.
     p.   cm.
  Contents: Quaestio disputata de virtutibus in communi—Quaestio disputata de virtutibus cardinalibus.
  ISBN 1-890318-20-5 (alk. paper)
  1.Virtue—Early works to 1800. I. Thomas, Aquinas, Saint, 1225?-1274. Quaestio disputata de virtutibus cardinalibus. II. Title.
  BV4630.T473 1998
  179'.9—dc21   98-20702
                                                            CIP
Paperbound published in 2009; ISBNs 978-1-58731-178-9; 1-58731-178-X

St. Augustine's Press
www.staugustine.net

Contents

Preface

In 1269, after teaching for ten years at various places in Italy, most recently at Santa Sabina in Rome, Thomas Aquinas returned to Paris for a second three-year stint as a regent professor of theology. In his late forties, Thomas was at the height of his powers. During his earlier stay in Paris, the main controversy he had faced was the criticism of the mendicants – the Franciscans and Dominicans – that came from the secular masters. Thomas wrote eloquently in defense of his Dominican vocation. These writings were on the margin of his main tasks as a master of theology. Those tasks are summed up as *legere, disputare, praedicare* – to comment on the sacred text, to engage in disputation with his peers, and to preach.

The Paris to which Thomas returned in 1269 was wracked by another controversy, one ignited by the youthful enthusiasms of some masters of philosophy, who seemed willing to waive questions as to how various philosophical positions related to their Christian faith.

"Didn't Aristotle say the world was eternal?"

"Yes, he did."

"But surely that conflicts with Genesis?"

"That's not important to us. We're doing philosophy."

These young masters, to put the most benign interpretation on it, wanted to pursue the study of philosophy without concern for how its claims related to the truths of faith. This tendency, called variously Latin Averroism and Heterodox Aristotelianism, met with strenuous criticism on the part of masters of theology. Stephen Tempier, the bishop of Paris, appointed a committee to look into the matter, and in 1270 a number of propositions were condemned. These were philosophical tenets which were taken to conflict with Christian faith.

In order to forestall a predictable late–twentieth-century reaction to this, several things must be understood. First, all of the disputants were Christians and thus accepted as true the tenets of

Christianity. Second, the principal criticism of Latin Averroism was that it seemed to regard as irrelevant the fact that a given proposition *p*, whose value, let us say, is "The world had no beginning," is incompatible with -*p*, that is, "In the beginning God made heaven and earth." Third, what came to be involved in the controversy was the legitimacy of a Christian's interest in Aristotle.

The Errors of Aristotle

This controversy generated lists of the "errors of Aristotle," of which three may be mentioned. First, the example just given, of the eternity of the world. Second, personal immortality of the human soul. Third, whether God has knowledge of the things of this world. If the world had a beginning in time, it is false to say that it has always existed. If man is called to an eternal destiny the nature of which will be decided by his actions on earth, it is false to say that death is the utter end of the human person. If God's eye is on the sparrow and the very hairs of our head are numbered, it is false to say that God does not and cannot know the events of this world. For a certain kind of critic, this prima-facie case sufficed, and the writings of Aristotle were regarded as sources of error and confusion rather than as a powerful help in the pursuit of truth. What was Thomas Aquinas's position on all this?

Thomas's interest in Aristotle dates from his pre-Dominican student days at the University of Naples and received a tremendous boost when, as a young Dominican, he studied with Albert the Great. Albert wrote a vast paraphrase of the writings of Aristotle and also commented on some Aristotelian works. While Thomas was his student, Albert commented on Aristotle's *Nicomachean Ethics*, and Thomas himself readied the work for distribution. From his own earliest writings, Thomas makes frequent reference to Aristotle and was, moreover, critical of such commentaries as those of Avicenna and Averroes that had come into Latin along with the text of Aristotle. But his earliest commentary on Aristotle dates from just before

Thomas's return to Paris. In Santa Sabina, in 1268, he at least began the commentary on Aristotle's *On the Soul*.

When Thomas entered the maelstrom of the Latin Averroist controversy, therefore, he was already extremely knowledgeable about the teachings of Aristotle. Indeed, there was reason to think that his own receptive attitude toward Aristotle was in the target area for critics of Latin Averroism. But the crisis that loomed was not simply a personal one. G. K. Chesterton, in his magnificent work on Thomas Aquinas, *The Dumb Ox*, goes unerringly to the heart of the matter. What was at issue was the relationship between faith and reason, between theology and philosophy, between Christianity and pagan culture. In this controversy, Chesterton sees Western civilization itself in the balance and credits Thomas with successfully navigating between the Scylla of insouciant incoherence, on the one hand, and the Charybdis of fideism on the other. The compatibility of faith and reason, the confidence that nothing the mind can discover can possibly be in conflict with what God has revealed, is the only rational policy for the Christian believer.

But what of the errors of Aristotle? It was of course of vital importance that Aristotle be correctly understood. This seems to have been Thomas's motivation for undertaking one of his most prodigious literary efforts, a close reading of the texts of Aristotle. The commentary, begun in Rome on Aristotle's *On the Soul,* was completed in Paris and was to be followed by ten others. Thomas died on March 7, 1274, and he is said to have stopped writing in his last year. From 1269 to 1273 amounts to five years. This was the period during which Thomas wrote the following commentaries: *On the Soul; On Sense and the Object of Sense; Physics; On Meteors; On Interpretation; Posterior Analytics; Nicomachean Ethics; Politics; Metaphysics; On the Heavens; On Generation and Corruption.* Not all of these are complete. They were written in Paris and in Naples, where Thomas went in 1272. If he had done nothing else during this period, these commentaries would count as one of the greatest achievements by a medieval master. But amazingly all of this was done on the margin of his magisterial work. Thomas was a theologian, and it was not part of his professorial task to comment on philosophical works. His lectures at the time were on books of the Bible – the epistles of St. Paul, the Gospel according to John, the Gospel according to Matthew, the Psalms. He also engaged in disputations. The two series of disputed questions that make up this book were products of this period of Thomas's life. And he was also at work on the Second Part of the Second Part of the *Summa theologiae*.

It was out of his profound understanding of Aristotle that Thomas addressed the issues of the Latin Averroism controversy. The eternity of the world? Yes, Aristotle assumed that the world had always been, and he was right to say that it makes no sense to hold that the world has come to be, *if coming to be is understood as it normally is.* Normally, becoming involves a thing that does not have a given characteristic acquiring it in the course of the change. That is, becoming presupposes a subject of the becoming, that to which the becoming is attributed. Obviously, this condition cannot be met in the case of the world – the presupposed subject would have to be part of the world – so Aristotle concluded that the world had always been. It was the theater of change, and could not itself be something that had come to be.

The Christian believes that God has created the world from nothing. Now nothing is not a pre-existent subject which turns into the world. Nothing is what there would be if God's causality were removed. Creation does not presuppose a subject. Creation is not a becoming. Is Thomas saying that Aristotle denied creation? Not quite. Thomas understands Aristotle to teach that everything other than the Prime Mover is dependent on the Prime Mover both in order to change and in order to exist. Thomas takes this to be grounds enough for saying that Aristotle's God is the creator of the world. So what is the difference, if it is not one between an uncreated and a created world?. The difference is between an eternally created world and a world that was created in time. Of course, Aristotle does not use the language of creation, but what he says comes down to the claim that the eternal world is dependent for its existence on the First Cause. Some thought this an incoherent claim. Thomas did not. God might have created the world from all eternity. We know that he did not because he told us so, in Genesis. Apart from that special information, it would be, Thomas holds, undecidable whether the world had been created eternally or in time.

The second and third "errors of Aristotle" mentioned above are misreadings of Aristotle, according to Thomas. Correctly understood, Aristotle supports the relevant Christian teachings. The message was clear. Aristotle, philosophy, is a precious resource for the believer. Philosophy meant for Thomas what it meant for Aristotle – all the knowledge there is, whatever we can learn by putting our minds to it. Thomas, unlike Aristotle, compared this with what St. Paul called the deposit of faith – all the truths God has vouchsafed to us by way of revelation. Theology is discourse that takes off from the starting points provided by revelation.

Aristotle's Ethics

Aristotle's moral teaching also came under fire during the controversy we have been discussing. This is hardly surprising, since we would seem to have a pretty clear conflict between what Aristotle has to say about the ultimate end in the *Ethics* and the Christian teaching on the meaning of human life.

Aristotle begins the *Ethics* with the remark that everything we do aims at some end which has the character of good; that is, it is fulfilling or perfecting of us. There are ends and ends, of course, and thus goods and goods. Sometimes we pursue something as a good and later ruefully acknowledge that it was not really so. A major task of the moral philosopher is to provide us with criteria for distinguishing between real and apparent goods. Without this distinction there would, of course, be no need for moral philosophy, the quest for what we should do. If every action is for the sake of an end, and every end is taken to be good, and there are no mistakes in the matter, then anything anybody does is good and everyone is as he ought to be. Remorse and regret prevent this easy solution.

A second important move in the *Ethics* is to observe that while some things are sought for the sake of something else, others are sought for their own sake. This linking of goods is pressed further when Aristotle observes that there are activities in which we pursue means to an end and that end is subservient to another end. For example, the cavalry involves a great cluster of activities, each set of which can be defined in terms of end and means, but they all aim at the point of having a cavalry in the first place, to field well-mounted, well-armed soldiers. The cavalry, along with other clusters – artillery, infantry, commissary, etc. – is aimed at the over-arching end of the military, victory. The general directs them all in order that the ultimate goal of victory can be attained.

Aristotle now makes the most dramatic move of all. Is there an over-riding purpose of human life, an ultimate end of all we do? Moral philosophy must articulate the ultimate end, and that is what Aristotle sets about doing. It is a magnificent effort. Suffice it to say that the ultimate end is happiness, and happiness is defined as a life lived according to virtue.

The Emergence of Virtue

What characterizes the human agent and sets him off from other agents is his mind and will. The human person pursues in action a project that he has first formulated in his mind. Since rational activity is peculiar to the human agent, the ultimate end of the human agent is performing rational activity well. Rational activity will be performed well when it aims at what is truly perfective of the human agent, viz., the ultimate end. Now if excellence of performance, *arete* – the term that is translated as virtue – is a way of performing rational activity, it seems that there is only one virtue, if "rational activity" always means the same thing. It is Aristotle's task, immediately after establishing the notion of ultimate end on the basis of the good of rational activity, to show that rational activity is of various kinds. This means that the excellent performance of rational activity does not always come to the same thing and that entails that there is a plurality of virtues.

Rational activity is first distinguished by Aristotle into the theoretical and practical uses of our mind. In the first case, the point of the effort is to arrive at the truth of the matter. In the case of practical thinking, thinking aims at the guidance of some activity other than thinking, as the sculptor's thinking guides his hands as he molds the clay. Not only is theoretical thinking distinguished from practical, each is seen to be divided into species. Sometimes the mind bears on principles, starting points, things which are of themselves true; sometimes the mind derives new truths from old, proceeding discursively; sometimes the mind relates the things it has come to know to their ultimate and first cause. Each of these three uses has a distinct excellence or virtue. They are, respectively, *understanding,* what Thomas calls *intellectus* and some have translated as intuition, *science,* and *wisdom.*

The virtues of the practical intellect are two: correct thinking with respect to things to be made, that is, *art;* and correct thinking with respect to things to be done, that is, *prudence.*

Speculative and practical uses of mind refer to rational activity essentially; but there is also a sense of rational activity that is derivative or participated. Insofar as our emotions can be schooled to respond to the direction of reason, they bear the imprint of reason. The concupiscible appetite is our instinctive tendency to seek the pleasure associated with food and drink and sexual activity. The irascible appetite is our instinctive tendency to attack or flee what harms us. A human being, whose life was dictated by these emotions, would not be guided by that which is distinctive of him, namely reason. Reason puts the pleasures and pains to which we respond emotionally into relation with our integral good. The pell-mell pursuit of pleasure is a recipe for personal misery. Training our emotions to respond to the direction of reason is a most difficult task. Its achievement is called virtue. The habit or disposition in the concupiscible appetite to respond to the direction of reason, and thus to pursue pleasures rationally, is called *temperance.* The habit or disposition to react rationally to threatened harm is called *courage.* These are rational activities, not because they are just as such activities of reason, but because they are activities which share in or participate in reason.

It takes some getting used to to think of science as a virtue, and there is a good reason for this. The term *virtue* is more familiarly applied to the imprint of reason on appetite, indeed, on sense appetite. Temperance and courage are the most obvious instances of virtue. Why? Aristotle defined virtue as that which makes the one having it good and makes his work good. The recurrence of "good" in the definition tells us that virtue will be found chiefly in appetite – the good is that which all things *seek*. Prudence, the virtue of practical intellect that governs what we do, is inextricably hooked up with temperance and courage. Prudence is in effect the search for and judgment of the way to achieve the end of the virtues in the primary sense. What does temperance require of me here and now? What does courage require of me in these circumstances? Such questions are pursued in the concrete – what is wanted is not an account on the level of generality but guidance here and now. Unless the concupiscible appetite bears the habitual imprint of obedience to reason, unless, that is, the person's appetitive disposition is determined to the good, practical reason will not be able to act effectively. If our sense appetite is disposed to pursue whatever pleasure promises, our thinking will be diverted to seeking means for realizing what we randomly want. In the best case, when the sense appetite bears the impress of reason, there is clearly a dependence on reason. There is, then, a virtuous circle involved.

The moral virtues – temperance and courage – presuppose correct practical reason, and correct practical reason presupposes the moral virtues. Aristotle's solution to this puzzle is endorsed by Thomas Aquinas. Practical reason both recognizes as true that our good lies in such and such *and* is able effectively to seek here and now means of achieving that good because of a track record of previous such efforts, an appetitive disposition or virtue.

A full account of the genesis of virtue would be lengthy indeed and would have to take into account the milieu in which we are brought up before the moral task comes into focus, the punishments and rewards that provide a predisposition to virtue or to vice, the heroes and heroines put before our imagination as models of excellent human behavior. Our main objective here is to provide the beginnings of an explanation as to why there is a plurality of virtues. There are intellectual virtues, and there are moral virtues. There are virtues of speculative intellect and virtues of practical intellect. The moral virtues, which have special claim to the term *virtue*, reside in appetite, in the concupiscible and irascible, but also in the intellectual appetite or will. We do not need to school ourselves to pursue our own good, but to take into account the good of those with whom we live does not come naturally. We must be schooled and school ourselves to pay attention to the goods of others as well as our own. This acquired disposition in the will is, of course, justice.

The Unity and Plurality of Virtues

Our discussion of the plurality of virtues was triggered by the definition of ultimate end. If it is the ultimate end of the human agent to perform well his distinctive activity, rational activity, and to do so is what is meant by excellence or virtue, then, if rational activity is revealed to be multiple in meaning, there will be a plurality of virtues. How do all of these virtues relate to a unified ultimate end? The human good would seem to be made up of all the particular goods aimed at by the various virtues. The virtues can be ranked in several ways. In terms of necessity, the moral virtues take precedence, since without them there would be personal and social chaos. In the *Ethics*, Aristotle treats moral virtues first and sees them as dispositive to and presupposed by the intellectual virtues. Thus, having treated the modes of temperance and courage, he discusses justice and then takes up the intellectual virtues, and first of all and preeminently prudence. But it is the perfection of the speculative use of our mind, the quest for truth, which is most essential to it; the practical use of mind extends reason beyond the category of knowing. The greatest perfection of rational activity is found in what Aristotle calls contemplation (*theoria*), whose preeminent object is the divine. While no one could devote himself exclusively to this, the society, and the person, whose dominant aim is the contemplation of the truth about the divine is the best.

Ultimate Ends?

Aristotle sought to lay out an ideal of human conduct that could be acquired by our own efforts and which would enable us to live well. By living well he meant living the life that is ours from birth to death. Aristotle seems almost embarrassed by questions relating to the state of souls after death rather than eager to pursue them, as Plato was. It is as if Aristotle were eschewing Platonic pie in the sky for the good that can be achieved in this life. This, more than any other single thing, seems to contrast Aristotle's notion of an ultimate end with the destiny of human persons that is revealed to us by Christianity.

The contrast is not diminished by pointing out that the supreme human good for Aristotle is contemplation of the divine. Magnificently true as this is, it is nonetheless an activity engaged in in this life, which is subject to unavoidable distractions and interruptions and limitations. The most exalted achievements of philosophical theology are a far cry from the beatific vision promised us after this life when we will see even as we are seen.

Now, obviously, there cannot be two ultimate ends of the human agent. By definition, the ultimate end is one. Consequently, if Aristotle has identified a certain good as our ultimate end, he means to say that it is sufficient. And if from a Christian point of view, what Aristotle has described is inadequate and insufficient, one of the claims must be false. That is, let p mean "Man's ultimate end consists of the virtuous activity that he performs in this life, preeminently in the contemplation of the divine." Then $-p$ will mean "Man's ultimate end consists in union with God after this life possible only because of supernatural grace." Thus, from the Christian point of view the Aristotelian account of ultimate end is false.

Perfect and Imperfect Happiness

Is this what Thomas Aquinas thinks? It is not. It is useful, in this matter, to remember his resolution of the controversy over the eternity of the world. Aristotle held that the world is eternal; Thomas believes that it is not, but he also knows that if God had wished he could have created an eternal world. Thus, the falsity of the philosophical position cannot be established philosophically; only on the basis of revelation is Thomas sure that the world is not eternal.

In the case of ultimate end, what Thomas finds in Aristotle is the recognition that the conception of ultimate end, which Aristotle has perfectly defined, is only imperfectly realized by the virtuous life that Aristotle describes. The notes of ultimate end are that it be sought for its own sake and not for the sake of something else, that it be sufficient, and that it cannot be lost once had. The ideal of ultimate end is only imperfectly realized by the good life Aristotle describes. For one thing, the virtues that have been acquired can be lost. If this is so, then while Aristotle's definition of ultimate end is a good one, that which realizes it, its instantiation by us, is imperfect. On this basis, Thomas is able to say that Aristotle, by his own statement, has described an imperfect happiness. And then, if there should be possible a perfect realization of ultimate end, the attainment of it will be perfect happiness.

Aristotle's notion of human happiness is not in conflict with the notion that human happiness consists in union with God for all eternity. The happiness possible in this life is an imperfect realization of the ultimate end; the beatific vision fulfills the notion of ultimate end perfectly. There is but one concept of ultimate, but there are two realizations of it, one imperfect, the other perfect.

Thus, Thomas sees a continuity between the end of life as philosophers depict it and the end of life that the believer pursues with the aid of supernatural grace.

Acquired and Infused Virtues

Virtue, as Aristotle spoke of it, is an acquired habit which relates the agent in a determinate way to the good attainable in this life. The dispositions of soul which relate one to the supernatural end are gifts, not acquisitions. They are infused into the soul. Thus, acquired virtues relate to man's end as naturally describable (which is an imperfect realization of the notion of ultimate end), whereas infused virtues relate to man's supernatural end.

In both the *Disputed Question on the Virtues in General* and in the *Disputed Question on the Cardinal Virtues,* Thomas treats of this distinction between acquired and infused virtues and their interplay in the moral agent. This contrast prompts him to descriptions of the acquired virtues which are sharper than they might otherwise have been. Throughout, the relation between the natural and supernatural, between moral philosophy and moral theology, are clarified, sometimes explicitly, often implicitly.

Virtue Ethics

For the past few decades there has been a resurgence of interest in what is called *Virtue Ethics.* As often as not this resurgence has been prompted by the realization that, apart from an acquired appetitive disposition, moral knowledge cannot be effective. Our moral character is a condition of our ability to see the demands of the good in particular circumstances. "As a man is, so does the end appear to him." In some manifestations, virtue ethics has seemed to be a relativizing of moral judgment to the subjective condition of the knower. There is no doubt that, in the crunch, in these circumstances here and now, the appetitive bent of the agent is decisive for the kind of concrete knowledge he has. Nonetheless, this ultimate practical discourse is the application to singular circumstances of truths recognized on the level of generality. As often as not, such moral generalization are true only for the most part. The maxim that one ought to return another's property has to be applied, and there are circumstances in which it would be folly to act on it. A discussion of such exceptions takes place at the level of universality. But beyond and behind such discourse there is a realm of first principles of the practical order, truths about action which are always and everywhere true. This is the realm of what Thomas calls *Natural Law* precepts or principles. It is the genius of Thomas's moral thought that it combines the exceptionless norms of natural law, the moral maxims which are true only by and large, and the singular judgment made here and now which brings all this universal knowledge into play but which has its certainty and truth from appetite's firm adherence to the good. The truth of practice lies in the judgment's conformity with rectified appetite.

The reader of the texts which follow will find light shed on many matters of moment for moral thought, both philosophical and theological. He will be reading texts that Thomas wrote at a time of great intellectual excitement and turmoil. That historical fact makes all the more remarkable the serene clarity of the exposition.

Disputed Question on the Virtues in General

THIRTEEN QUESTIONS are addressed.

Article 1
Are virtues habits?

It seems that they are not, but are rather acts.

1. For Augustine says in the *Retractions* that the good use of free will is a virtue. But the use of free will is an act. Therefore, virtue is an act.

2. Moreover, no one is owed a reward except by reason of an act. But a reward is owed to everyone possessing virtue, because who-

ever dies in charity attains happiness. Therefore, virtue is a merit. But merit is an act. Therefore, virtue is an act.

3. Moreover, the more something in us is like God, the better it is. But we are most like God insofar as we actually are, because he is pure act. Therefore, act is what is best in us. But virtues are what is best in us, as Augustine says in *On free will*. Therefore, virtues are acts.

4. Moreover, perfection in this life answers to perfection in the next. But the perfection of heaven is an act, namely, happiness, that consists in activity, according to the Philosopher. Therefore, the perfection of this life, which is virtue, is an act.

5. Moreover, contraries belong to the same genus and mutually exclude one another. But an act of sin expels virtue because of its opposition to it. Therefore, virtue is in the genus of act.

6. Moreover, the Philosopher says in *On the heavens* 1 that virtue is the utmost of a potency. But the utmost of a potency is act. Therefore, virtue is an act.

7. Moreover, the rational part is more noble and perfect than the sensitive part. But no habit or quality mediates between the sensitive part and its activity. Therefore, in the intellective part, there should not be habits by the mediation of which the intellective part has its perfect operation.

8. Moreover, the Philosopher says in *Physics 7* that virtue is the disposition of the perfected to the best. But the best is act, and a disposition is in the same genus as that to which it disposes. Therefore, virtue is an act.

9. Moreover, Augustine says in *On the customs of the Church* that virtue is the order of love. But order, as he says in *The city of God* xix, disposes what is equal and unequal in a thing to their places. Therefore, virtue is a disposition and not a habit.

10. Moreover, habit is a quality difficult to change. But virtue is easily removed, because it is taken away by one act of mortal sin. Therefore, virtue is not a habit.

11. Moreover, if we need certain habits, which are virtues, we need them either for natural activities or for meritorious ones, which are supernatural. But not for the natural, because if any nature, sensible or insensible, can perfect its activity without a habit, a fortiori rational nature can do this. Likewise, not for meritorious activities,

because God works these in us, Philippians 2, 13, "who works in you both the will and the performance." Therefore, virtues are in no way habits.

12. Moreover, any agent that acts thanks to its form acts according to the demands of that form, as the warm always acts by heating. Therefore, if there were in the mind some habitual form called virtue, the one having virtue would have to act virtuously, which is false, because then anyone having virtue would be confirmed (in the good). Therefore, virtues are not habits.

13. Moreover, habits are in powers that they might have ease of action. But we do not need something facilitating the acts of virtues, as is clear. For they consist chiefly in choice and will. But nothing easier than what is constituted in the will. Therefore, virtues are not habits.

14. Moreover, the effect cannot be nobler than its cause. But if virtue is a habit, it will be the cause of the act, which is nobler than the habit. Therefore, it does not seem fitting that virtue should be a habit.

15. Moreover, the mean and extremes are in the same genus. But moral virtue is a mean between passions; but passions are in the genus of acts; therefore . . .

ON THE CONTRARY. 1. Virtue, according to Augustine, is a good quality of mind. But it can only be in the first species [of quality], which is habit. Therefore, virtue is a habit.

2. Moreover, the Philosopher says in *Ethics* 2 that virtue is a habit of choosing in the mind.

3. Moreover, virtues exist in sleepers, because they are only taken away by mortal sin. But there are no virtuous acts of sleepers, since they do not have the use of free will. Therefore, virtues are not acts.

RESPONSE. It should be said that virtue, given its meaning, designates the completion of a power; so strength means that thanks to which a thing, by the complete power it has, can bring about its impetus or motion. Virtue, according to its name, points to the perfection of a power. Hence, the Philosopher said in *On the heavens* 1 that virtue is the utmost reach of the power of the thing. But because potency is said with reference to act, a potency is fulfilled when it has its complete activity. And because activity is the end of the agent, since any thing is for the sake of its own activity as for its proximate end, as the Philosopher says in *On the heavens 1,* a thing is good insofar as it has a complete ordering to its end. Hence, virtue makes the one having it good and makes his work good, as is said in *Ethics* 2, and thus it is evident that it is the disposition of the perfected for the best, as is said in *Metaphysics* 7.

All of these pertain to the virtue of anything. For the virtue of a horse is what makes him and his activity good; similarly the virtue of a rock or a man or any other thing. But as potencies differ so does the mode of their complexity. For some powers only act, others are only acted upon or moved, yet others are both acted upon and act on others.

The potency which only acts does not require, in order to be a principle of action, that anything be brought to bear on it; hence, the virtue of such a potency is nothing other than the potency itself. Such is the divine power, the agent intellect and natural powers; that is why the virtues of such powers are not habits but the potencies themselves as complete in themselves.

But those powers which both act and are acted upon and which are so moved that they are not determined to a single object, act in a manner that is, in a way, rational. Such powers act insofar as something is added to them, not just in a manner of a passion, but as a form which abides in the subject but which does not determine the subject to a single object – if that were so, the power would not have dominion over its act. Hence, in *Ethics 3* it is said that sense is not the principle of any act, and these powers are perfected in their acts only thanks to something superadded, which, however, is not in them in the manner of a form abiding in its subject but only in the manner of passion, as the species (image) in the pupil. Hence, the virtues of these powers are not habits but rather the power themselves, insofar as they are actually acted upon by their agents. Those powers act and are acted upon that are so moved by their agents that they are not determined to one. Action belongs to them as to powers which in a sense are rational, and these powers are completed in acting by something superadded, which is not in them in the manner of a passion alone but in the manner of an abiding form remaining in the subject, in such a way, however, that by it the power is not necessitated to one, since then the power would not have dominion over its act. The virtues of these powers are not the powers themselves, nor passion, as with sensitive powers, nor qualities acting necessarily, like the qualities of natural things. Rather they are habits thanks to which one can act when he likes, as the Commentator says in *On the Soul 3*. And Augustine in *On the conjugal good* says that habit is that whereby one acts when time permits.

Therefore, it is clear that virtues are habits and how habits differ from the second and third species of quality. How do they differ from the fourth species? Figure as such is not ordered to act.

From all of which it can be seen that we need the habit of virtues for three things. First, for uniformity in operation; for what depends solely on operation is easily altered unless it is stabilized by some habitual inclination.

Second, in order that perfect operation be promptly at hand. For unless the rational power is in some way inclined to one [of contraries] by habit, when we act it will always be necessary for the activity to be preceded by inquiry, something obvious in one who does not yet have the habit of science or one wishing to act virtuously who does not have the habit of virtue. Hence, the Philosopher in *Ethics* 6 says that things done right away are from habit.

Third, in order that perfect activity might be pleasantly accomplished. This results from habit which, since it acts in the manner of a kind of nature, makes the activity proper to it, as it were, natural and, consequently, delightful. For fittingness is a cause of delight. Hence, the Philosopher in *Ethics* 2 gives as a mark of habit the delight taken in acting.

Ad. 1. It should be said that virtue, like power, is understood in two ways. In one way, materially, as when we say that what we can do is our power or strength; and thus Augustine calls the good use of free will a virtue. Second, essentially, and thus neither power nor virtue is an act.

Ad 2. It should be said that to deserve or merit is taken in two ways. First, properly, and thus it is nothing other than the performance of some action by which one justly acquires a reward for himself. Second, improperly, and thus any condition that makes a man in any way worthy is called merit, as when we say that the mien of Priam merits command since it was worthy of command. So a reward ought to follow on merit, and is in a way owed to the habitual quality by which one is made worthy of reward, and thus it is owed to baptized infants. It is also owed to actual merit, and thus it is not owed to virtue but to the act of virtue. Yet even to little ones it is given as by reason of actual merit, insofar as by the merit of Christ the sacrament has the efficacy, by which one is regenerated to life.

Ad 3. It should be said that Augustine says that the virtues are the highest goods, not absolutely, but of their kind, just as fire is said to be the most subtle body. Hence, it does not follow that there is nothing in us better than these virtues but that they are numbered among things that are the highest goods of their kind.

Ad 4. It should be said that just as in life there is a habitual perfection which is a virtue, and the actual perfection which is the act of virtue, so too in heaven happiness is actual perfection, proceeding from some consummate habit. Hence, the Philosopher too in *Ethics* 1 says that happiness is an activity in accord with perfect virtue.

Ad 5. It should be said that vicious acts directly remove the act of virtue because of contrariety, but they remove the habit of virtue only incidentally insofar as it is separated from the cause of infused virtue, namely, from God. Hence, in Isaiah 59, 2: "But your iniquities have divided between you and your God." That is why acquired virtues are not taken away by one vicious act.

Ad 6. It should be said that that definition of the Philosopher can be understood in two ways. In one way, materially, such that by virtue we understand that of which the virtue is capable, which is the utmost of which the power is capable, as the virtue of one who can carry a hundred pounds is his insofar as he can carry a hundred pounds, not sixty. Second, it can be understood essentially, and thus virtue means the utmost reach of the power because it signifies the completion or fulfillment of the power, whether or not what completes the power is other than it.

Ad 7. It should be said that sensitive and rational powers do not get the same account.

Ad 8. It should be said that a disposition for something is that through which something is moved to achieve something. But motion sometimes has its term in the same genus, as quality in the case of alteration as such; hence the disposition to that term is always of the same genus as the term. Sometimes, however, it has a term in another genus, as when the term of alteration is a substantial form, and thus the disposition is not always of the same genus as that to which it disposes, as heat is a disposition to the substantial form of heat.

Ad 9. It should be said that disposition is said in three ways. First, as heat is the disposition for the form of fire. Second, as that by which an agent is disposed to act, as speed is the disposition to run. Third, disposition means the ordering of things to one another, and Augustine takes disposition in this sense. Disposition in the first sense is contrasted with habit, whereas in the second sense, virtue itself is a disposition.

Ad 10. It should be said that nothing is so stable that it is not immediately undone when its cause is removed. It is no wonder then that if union with God is taken away by mortal sin, infused virtue should go. Nor does this impugn its stability, which can only be understood in terms of its cause remaining.

Ad 11. It should be said that we need habit for both operations. For natural operations for the three reasons given above; for meritorious acts too, in order that the natural power can be elevated by the infused habit to that which is above nature. Nor is this affected by the fact that God works in us, because he so acts in us that we too act, hence we need a habit whereby we can act sufficiently.

Ad 12. It should be said that every form is received in its subject in the manner of the one receiving. But it is proper to the rational power that it is capable of opposites and has dominion over its act. Hence, the rational power is not forced to do the same thing by the habitual form acquired, but it can act or not act.

Ad 13. It should be said that what is a matter of choice alone can easily come about in one way or another, but it is no easy matter for it to come about as it should, that is, expeditiously, firmly, pleasantly. For that we need the habits of the virtues.

Ad 14. It should be said that any motion, whether of man or beast, that begins from scratch is produced by some mover, and depends on something that exists prior, and thus a habit does not elicit an act from itself except insofar as it is stirred by some agent.

Ad 15. It should be said that virtue is a mean between passions, not as if it were some middle passion, but as an action that brings about a mean between passions.

Article 2
Is Augustine's definition of virtue all right?

His definition is: Virtue is a good quality of mind whereby we live rightly, which no one misuses and that God works in us without us.
This does not seem right.

1. Virtue is a good. If it is good, this is either by its own goodness or that of another. If another's, we have an infinite regress. If by its own, virtue is the first goodness because only the first goodness is good of itself.

2. Moreover, what is common to every being ought not be put in the definition of any one of them, but the good, which is convertible with being, is common to every being and thus ought not be put into the definition of virtue.

3. Moreover, the good is in the moral as it is in the natural, but good and evil in natural things do not constitute species. Therefore, good ought not be put into the definition as the specific difference of virtue.

4. Moreover, the difference is not included in the definition of the genus. But good is included in the definition of quality, as is being. Therefore, it ought not be added to the definition of virtue, as when it is said that virtue is a good quality of mind, etc.

5. Moreover, good and evil are opposites. But evil does not constitute any species, since it is a privation. No more then should good. Therefore, it ought not be put into the definition of virtue as a constitutive difference.

6. Moreover, because good is broader than quality, one quality does not differ from another because it is good. Therefore, good ought not be put in the definition of virtue as a difference of quality or virtue.

7. Moreover, nothing comes to be from two acts. But good implies an act and so too does quality. Therefore, it is not well said that virtue is a good quality.

8. Moreover, what is predicated abstractly is not predicated concretely: Whiteness is a color but it is not colored. But goodness is predicated abstractly of virtue, and thus is not predicated of it concretely. Therefore, it is not right to say that virtue is a good quality.

9. Moreover, no difference is predicated abstractly of species, and that is why Avicenna says that man is not rationality but rational. But virtue is goodness. Therefore, goodness is not a difference of virtue, and it is not right to say that virtue is a good quality.

10. Moreover, evil in the moral order is vice. Therefore, good in the moral order is the same as virtue. But then good ought not be put in the definition of virtue, because then the thing would be defined by itself.

11. Moreover, mind pertains to intellect. But virtue looks rather to appetite. Therefore, it is not right to say that virtue is a good quality of mind.

12. Moreover, according to Augustine mind names the higher part of the soul. But some virtues are in the lower powers. Therefore, it is not right to put 'good quality of mind' in the definition of virtue.

13. Moreover, a power not the essence is called the subject of virtue. But mind seems to name the essence of soul, because Augustine says that in mind are intelligence, memory, and will. Therefore, mind ought not be put in the definition of virtue.

14. Moreover, that which is proper to species ought not be put in the definition of the genus. But rectitude is proper to justice. Therefore, rectitude ought not be put in the definition of virtue as when it is called a good quality of mind whereby one lives rightly.

15. Moreover, for living things to be is to live. But virtue does not perfect with respect to existence but with respect to acts. Therefore, it is not right that it be called that whereby one lives rightly.

16. Moreover, whoever takes pride in something, uses it badly. But one can be proud of virtues. Therefore, one can use virtue badly.

17. Moreover, in *On free will* Augustine says that it is only the greatest goods that no one uses badly. But virtue is not among the greatest goods, since the greatest is desired for its own sake, and that is not the case with virtue, which is sought for the sake of something else, namely, happiness. That being so, it is not right to include in the definition, 'which no one uses badly.'

18. Moreover, a thing is generated, nourished, and grows from the same thing. But virtue is nourished and increased by our acts because a lessening of cupidity is an increase in charity. Therefore, vir-

tue comes about from our own acts, and 'what God works in us without us' is wrongly put into its definition.

19. Moreover, the removal of an impediment counts as an efficient cause. But free will is in a way the removal of an impediment to virtue. Therefore, it is in a way its cause, and it is not right to say that God causes virtue in us without us.

20. Moreover, Augustine says: Who created you without your help will not justify you without your help. Therefore . . .

21. Moreover, that definition seems to belong to grace. But virtue and grace are not one and the same thing. Therefore, this is not a good definition of virtue.

RESPONSE. It should be said that this would be the definition of virtue even if that last clause were omitted, and it fits every human virtue. For, as has been said, virtue perfects a power with respect to perfect act. But perfect act is the end of the power or of the one acting. Hence, virtue makes both the power and the agent good, as was said earlier. Thus, in the definition of virtue there is something that pertains to the perfection of the act and something that pertains to the perfection of the power or agent.

Two things are required for the perfection of the act: first, that the act be right; second, that the habit cannot be the principle of the contrary of the act. That which is the principle of both a good and a bad act cannot as such be the perfect principle of the good act, for habit is the perfection of the power. That is why it must be the principle only of the good act and in no way of a bad. Hence the Philosopher in *Ethics* 6 says that opinion, which bears on both the true and false, is not a virtue, whereas science, which bears only on the true, is. The first condition is indicated by 'whereby one lives rightly,' and the second by 'which no one uses badly.'

In order for virtue to make the subject good, three things must be taken into account. The *subject* itself, and this is indicated when he says 'of mind,' since human virtue can be in man only insofar as he is a man. The *perfection* of intellect is indicated by the inclusion of 'good,' because good follows on the ordering to end. The *mode* of inherence is designated by the mention of 'quality,' because virtue cannot inhere in the manner of a passion, but rather in the manner of a habit, as has been said above.

The perfection of intellect is called 'good' because good means the order to the end. The mode of inherence is designated by 'quality' because virtue does not inhere in the manner of a passion but in the manner of a habit, as was said above. All these things belong to both moral and intellectual virtue, whether theological or acquired or infused. When Augustine adds 'what God works in us without us,' this pertains to infused virtue only.

Ad 1. It should be said that just as accidents are called beings, not because they subsist, but because by them something is, so virtue is not called good because it itself is good, but because by it something else is good. That is why virtue need not be good by another goodness, as if it were informed by another goodness.

Ad 2. It should be said that the good that is convertible with being is not put in the definition of virtue, but the good that is specific to the moral act.

Ad 3. It should be said that acts are distinguished according to the form of the agent, as heating and freezing are. But good and evil are, as it were, the form and object of will: The agent always impresses its form on what it acts upon, as does the mover on the moved. Therefore, moral acts, which have will as their principle, are distinguished specifically into the good and bad. But the principle of natural activities is form, not the end, and that is why natural activities are not distinguished into good and bad as species, though that is how it is in moral acts.

Ad 4. It should be said that moral goodness is not included in the understanding of quality, so the argument is not relevant.

Ad 5. It should be said that evil does not constitute a species by reason of privation, but by reason of that which sustains the privation, because it is incompatible with the notion of good, and from this it takes its species.

Ad 6. It should be said that this objection proceeds from the good of nature, not from the good of morals, which is put in the definition of virtue.

Ad 7. It should be said that goodness does not imply another goodness than that of virtue itself, as is clear from the foregoing. In its essence virtue is a quality; hence, it is obvious that good and quality do not indicate different acts, but one.

Ad 8. It should be said that this does not obtain in transcendentals which apply to every being, for essence is being and goodness is good and unity is one, but we cannot say that whiteness is white. The reason is that anything the intellect grasps falls under the notion of being, and consequently under the good and one. Hence, essence and goodness cannot be understood otherwise than under the notes of good and one and being, which is why goodness is said to be good and unity one.

[*In the absence of Thomas's response to the remaining objections, Vincent de Castro Novo, O.P. supplied the following responses.*]

Ad 9. It should be said that difference, like genus, is predicated of species essentially, not denominatively. Therefore, if the species is subsistent and compositive, it is not predicated of the difference abstractly, but concretely. The concrete names of composite substances signify the composites, and these are properly put into a category, as species and genera, for example, man and animal. Therefore, if the difference must be predicated of such a species essentially, it should be signified concretely; otherwise it would not be said of the whole species. But if the species is a simple form – think of accidents, the concrete names of which, like 'white' and 'black,' are not placed in a category as species or genera, save by way of reduction, but only as abstractly signified, e.g., whiteness, music, justice, and, generally, virtue – then either the genus or difference abstractly signified is predicated of them, and that is why, just as virtue is essentially a quality, so it is essentially the goodness of reason or of the moral.

Ad 10. It should be said that the moral good is said of the act, of the habit, and of the object. Similarly, moral evil is said of a bad act which is a sin and of a bad habit which is a vice. Hence, virtue is that which makes the one having it good and makes his act good with moral goodness; similarly vice is what makes the one having it evil and makes his act evil with moral badness. Therefore, moral evil is not the same as vice, since vice names a habit, whereas moral evil is said of habit and act and object. By parity of reasoning the moral good is not identical with virtue, since moral goodness is said of the act as well.

Three things can be considered in virtue.

First, that which the essence of virtue directly implies, and thus virtue implies a certain disposition whereby a thing is well and fittingly disposed given its nature. Hence, the Philosopher says in *Physics* 7 that "virtue is a disposition that perfects for the best, and I mean the perfected which is disposed according to nature." In this way, vice is opposed to virtue because it implies a disposition by which a thing is disposed to that which does not befit its nature. Hence, Augustine says in *On free will* 3: "When you see something that is lacking to the perfection of a nature, call it a vice, because the vice of a thing seems to be that by which it is indisposed to that which befits its nature."

Second, is that which follows on its essence which virtue signifies by way of consequence; in this way, virtue implies a goodness that makes the one having it good. For a thing's good consists in this, that it is appropriately disposed with respect to its nature. This is what virtue brings about, as has been said, which is why it is an ordered, that is, a good action. For virtue is ordered by reason to the good or fitting act. Hence, virtue is the perfection of a power with reference to act and not only makes the one having it good but makes his act good as well. In this way, virtue is opposed to sin, which properly signifies an inordinate act.

From this it is clear that the vicious habit, evil, and sin can be called the evil of morals, and every virtue the good of morals, and not the reverse.

Ad 11. It should be said that mind is taken here to stand for the rational powers and thus means both intellect and will: will is essentially a rational power. Virtues are found both in intellect and in the affective part. Intellectual virtues give the capacity of acting well but not the good use of that capacity, whereas moral virtues, which are virtues simply speaking, give to the affective both the capacity of acting well and its good use, bringing it about that one uses the capacity well and rightly. For example, justice not only gives one the capacity to perform just acts but also makes one act justly. Grammar, on the other hand, only gives the capacity to speak correctly and well, but does not bring it about that a man always speaks well. One well versed in grammar can make grammatical mistakes, for example, solecisms. From which it is clear that virtue refers both to the appetitive and the intellective powers, since both are included in mind.

Ad 12. It should be said that mind means a type of power which is the principle of the acts over which man has dominion, and these are properly called human acts. Reason and will are such powers, for they are what first move and command the act over which man has dominion, and they are said to be essentially rational. But the irascible and concupiscible are principles of human acts insofar as they participate in reason, but as moved movers. For they are moved by the higher appetite insofar as they obey it, and thus, insofar as they participate in reason and are so fashioned as to obey this, it is clear that reason and will are the first principle of the human act as moving and commanding, and sensitive appetite is a secondary principle as a moved mover, and such powers are meant by mind and can be the subject of virtue.

Again, mind implies a power that is rational either essentially or by way of participation. The irascible and concupiscible are rational powers by way of participation, and can be the subject of virtue insofar as they participate in mind.

Ad 13. It should be said that mind signifies what is highest in the soul's power. Hence, since the divine image is found in that which is highest in us, it must be said that image does not pertain to soul in its essence but only according to mind which names its highest power. Thus, insofar as it is image mind names a power of the soul and not its essence; thus mind includes those powers which in their acts recede from matter and the conditions of matter. In mind are included intelligence, will, and memory, not as accidents of a subject, but as parts of a whole.

Ad 14. It should be said that rectitude is of two kinds. There is one which is special and is constitutive with reference to external things which come into man's use and are the proper matter of justice. There is another that is general and implies an order to the fitting end and to divine law, and this is common to every virtue and enters into the definition of virtue.

Ad 15. It should be said that "to live" is taken in two ways. In one way for the existence of the living thing, and thus it pertains to the essence of the soul which is the principle of being in living things. Hence, the Philosopher in *On the soul* 2 says that for living things to exist is for them to live. In that sense, 'live' does not enter into the definition of virtue. It is taken in another sense for the activity of the living thing, insofar as understanding and sensing are ways of being alive. Hence, it is that the activity that is most pleasurable and most occupies one is called his life, and the Philosopher says in *Metaphysics* 1 that the human race lives by art and reasoning, that is, acts. It is in this sense that life is put in the definition of virtue, which by virtue a man rightly acts.

Ad 16. It should be said that badly using virtue can mean two things. First, when it is taken as an object, and then one can badly use it when he thinks ill of virtue or hates or takes pride in it. Second, as the elicitive principle of bad use, such that a bad act is elicited by virtue, and in this sense one cannot use virtue badly. For virtue is a habit always inclining to the good, since every virtue gives the capacity of acting well and also give good use and not just the capacity and insure that one uses the capacity well. Of this kind are the virtues of the appetitive power, as justice not only makes a man ready to do just things but brings it about that he acts justly.

Ad 17. It should be said that only the greatest goods are such that one cannot use them badly as objects since they are of themselves desirable and can be hated by no one. But virtues, which are not the greatest goods, one can use badly as objects, as was said above; but they cannot be used badly as being the elicitive principle. It is not necessary that what one cannot use badly as an elicitive principle should be the highest good. It can also be said, according to Augustine, that virtue is numbered among the highest goods insofar as through it man is ordered to the highest good, which is God, and for this reason no one uses virtue badly.

Ad 18. It should be said that just as acquired virtues increase and are nourished by the acts that caused them, so infused virtues are increased by the act of God by whom they are caused. Our acts dispose for an increase of charity and the infused virtues, as a man at the outset, by doing what is natural to him, prepares and disposes himself to receive charity from God. Subsequent acts can merit an increase in charity because they presuppose charity, which is the principle of merit. But no one can merit that he might receive charity in the first place, because there can be no merit without charity. From which it is clear that charity and the other infused virtues are not actively increased by acts, but only as disposing and meriting; they are actively increased by the action of God who perfects and conserves the charity that he first infused.

Ad 19. It should be said that sin is what prevents virtue. Free will without the action of God is not of itself sufficient to remove sin, because God alone effectively wipes away iniquity and rids of sin. The Holy Spirit moving the mind of man more or less according to his own will provides any disposition or preparation or effort of free will that precedes charity. For the remission of sin is not without grace, and thus in Romans 3, 24, we read, "They are justified freely by his grace."

Ad 20. It should be said that infused virtue is caused in us by God without our doing anything but not without our consent; thus, God does not justify us unless we are consenting because it is by an act of free will that we consent to God's justice when we are justified. That movement is not formally the cause of justifying grace, but its effect, such that the whole operation pertains to grace and to God, which effectively justifies by infusing grace. The things done by us of which we are the cause God causes in us but not without our acting, for he acts in every will and nature.

Ad 21. It should be said that the definition of virtue, properly understood, does not apply to grace, for grace is an instance of the first species of quality. It is not a habit like virtue, nor is it immediately ordered to activity; rather, it is like a relation which confers a kind of spiritual and divine existence on the soul and is presupposed by the infused virtues as their cause and root. Grace is to the essence of soul as health is to the body. That is why Chrysostom in a homily said that grace is the health of mind. It is not counted among the sciences or virtues or the other qualities that philosophers have enumerated because they only knew those accidents of the soul which are ordered to acts proportioned to human nature.

Virtue, therefore, is essentially a habit, but grace is not a habit but rather a supernatural participation in the divine nature according to which we become consorts of the divine nature, as is said in 1 Peter 2, by the reception of which we are said to be reborn as the sons of God. Hence, just as the natural light of reason is root and cause of acquired virtue, so the light of grace, which is the participation in the divine nature in the very essence of the soul by means of a kind of indwelling, is the root and cause of infused virtue.

Again, virtue is a good quality which makes the one having it good: For this goodness which virtue confers on the one having it is the goodness of perfection in relation to activity of which it is the immediate principle. But the goodness that grace confers on the soul is the goodness of perfection not immediately in relation to activity but to a certain spiritual and divine existence, thanks to which those having grace are said to be made like God and thus sons of God freely by his grace. Hence, the 'good' put in the definition of virtue indicates a fittingness to some pre-existent nature, essential or participated. This good is not attributed to grace, save as to the principle and cause of such goodness in man.

Mind as it is put in the definition of virtue means a power of the soul, which is the subject of virtue; but potency in the definition of grace means the essence of the soul, which is the subject of grace.

Again 'to live' as put in the definition of virtue means activity of which virtue is the immediate principle, but life as it is attributed to grace means a certain divine existence of which it is the immediate principle, and not activity to which it is only ordered through the mediation of virtue.

Again, virtue is called the disposition of what is best on the part of one already perfected, because it perfects the power with respect to the activity whereby a thing achieves its end. Grace is not the disposition of the perfected to the best in this way, first, because it does not primarily perfect the power but the essence, and also because it does not have activity as its proper effect, but rather something divine. From all of which it is clear that the definition of virtue does not apply to grace.

This is the end of the additions.

Article 3

Can a power of the soul be the subject of virtue?

It seems that it cannot.

1. According to Augustine, virtue is that whereby we live well. But to live follows on the essence of the soul, not on a power of it. Therefore, there cannot be a virtue of a power of the soul.

2. Moreover, the existence of grace is more perfect than that of nature. The existence of nature is through the essence of soul, which is more noble than the powers, being their principle. Therefore, the existence of grace, which is through the virtues, is not through the powers, so power cannot be the subject of virtue.

3. Moreover, an accident cannot be a subject. But a power of the soul is in the genus of accident, for natural ability and inability belong to the second species of quality. Therefore, a power of the soul cannot be the subject of virtue.

4. Moreover, if one power of the soul could be the subject of virtue, any could, since any power of the soul is hostile to vice, against which the virtues are ordered. But not just any power of the soul can be the subject of virtue, as will be clear below. Therefore, the subject of virtue cannot be a power.

5. Moreover, active principles such as heat and cold found in the natures of other agents are not subjects; but the powers of the soul are active principles, for they are the principles of the activities of the soul. Therefore, they cannot be the subjects of other accidents.

6. Moreover, the subject of a power is the soul. Therefore, if a power is the subject of another accident, by parity of reasoning that accident will be the subject of another accident, and so it will go on indefinitely, which is absurd. Therefore, the power of the soul is not the subject of virtue.

7. Moreover, it is said in *Posterior Analytics* 1 that there is no quality of quality. But the power of the soul belongs to the second species of quality; and virtue is in the first species of quality. Therefore, the power of the soul cannot be the subject of virtue.

ON THE CONTRARY. 1. That whose action it is, is the principle of the action. But the actions of the virtues are of the powers. Therefore, the virtues are as well.

2. Moreover, the Philosopher says in *Ethics* 1 that the intellectual virtues are essentially rational, but the moral virtues are rational by way of participation. But what is rational either essentially or by participation names a power of the soul. Therefore, the powers of the soul are not subject of virtue.

RESPONSE. It should be said that a subject relates to accident in three ways. In one way, as providing it sustaining power, for the accident does not exist of itself, but is supported by the subject. In another way, as potency to act, for the subject is subject to the accident as to an active power, which is why the accident is called a form. In a third way, as cause to effect, for the subject principles are, per se, principles of the accident.

With respect to the first, one accident cannot be the subject of another accident. For, since no accident exists of itself, it cannot provide sustaining power to another, unless perhaps it were said that it sustains another accident insofar as it itself is sustained by the subject.

With respect to the other two, one accident relates to another in the manner of a subject insofar as it is in potency to the other, as the diaphanous relates to light and surface to color. One accident can also be the cause of another, as the moist is of taste, and in this way one accident can be the subject of another. It is not that one accident can provide sustainment to the other, but that the subject receives one accident by the mediation of the other. It is in this way that a power of the soul is said to be the subject of a habit. The habit is to the power as act to potency, since potency taken as such is undetermined and is only determined to this or that by a habit. And acquired habits are caused by the principles of the powers. That is why the powers must be called the subjects of virtue, since virtue is in the soul by the mediation of the power.

Ad 1. It should be said that living as it occurs in the definition of virtue pertains to action, as was said earlier.

Ad 2. It should be said that spiritual existence is from grace, not from virtue, for grace is the principle of existing spiritually, but virtue is the principle of acting spiritually.

Ad 3. It should be said that the power is not of itself a subject, but only insofar as it is sustained by the soul.

Ad 4. It should be noted that we are speaking now of human virtues. Therefore, powers which cannot in any way be human, since the sway of reason does not extend to them, cannot be subjects of virtue, e.g., the vegetative powers. However, whatever resistance arises from such powers is mediated through sense appetite to which the sway of reason extends and which can therefore be called human and be the subject of human virtue.

Ad 5. It should be said that only the agent intellect and the powers of the vegetable soul are active powers of soul, and they are not subjects of any habit. But the passive powers of the soul are the principles of acts only insofar as they are moved by their active causes.

Ad 6. It should be said that it is not necessary to regress infinitely, because we will come to an accident that is not in potency to another accident.

Ad 7. It should be said that there is no quality of quality such that one quality would be the per se subject of another, which is not the case here, as was said above.

Article 4

Whether the irascible and concupiscible can be the subjects of virtue

It seems that they cannot.

1. Contraries come to be in the same thing. But mortal sin is contrary to virtue and cannot exist in sensuality, whose parts are the irascible and concupiscible. Therefore, the irascible and concupiscible cannot be subjects of virtue.

2. Moreover, habit and act belong to the same power. But the principal act of virtue is choice, according to the Philosopher in the *Ethics*, but this is not an act of either the concupiscible or the irascible. So there cannot be habits of virtue in the irascible and concupiscible.

3. Moreover, no corruptible thing is the subject of what is perpetual; hence Augustine proves that the soul is perpetual, because it is the subject of truth which is perpetual. But the irascible and concupiscible, like the other powers of the soul, do not survive the body as, or so it has seemed to some, the virtues do. For justice is perpetual and immortal, as is said in Wisdom I, 15, and for the same reason this could be said of all virtues. Therefore, the irascible and concupiscible cannot be the subject of virtues.

4. Moreover, the irascible and concupiscible have bodily organs. Therefore, if there are virtues of the irascible and concupiscible, they are in a bodily organ and can be grasped by the imagination or fancy. But then they are not perceptible by mind alone, as Augustine says of justice, which is a rectitude perceptible only by mind.

5. If it should be said that the irascible and concupiscible can be the subject of virtue insofar as they participate in reason in some way, the response is that they are said to participate in reason insofar as they are ordered by reason. But the ordering of reason cannot provide sustaining power to a virtue, since it is not something subsistent. Therefore, the irascible and concupiscible cannot be the subject of virtue because they participate in reason.

6. Moreover, the apprehensive and sensitive powers serve reason as do the irascible and concupiscible, which pertain to sense appetite,

do. But there is no virtue in any of the apprehensive powers of sense. Therefore, not in the irascible and concupiscible.

7. Moreover, if the order of reason can be participated in by the irascible and concupiscible, the rebellion of sensuality would be diminished, and these two powers would be contained by reason. But this rebellion is not infinite, since sensuality is a finite power and there cannot be an infinite act of a finite power. Thus, it could completely stamp out this rebellion, since any finite thing is removed if a little bit is taken away again and again, as the Philosopher makes clear in *Physics* 1. But then sensuality in this life could be totally cured, which is impossible.

8. If it should be said that God, who infuses virtue, could completely remove this rebellion even if it cannot be done by us, the response is that man is what he is insofar as he is rational, since his species is formed from this. To the degree then that anything in man is subject to reason, it belongs to human nature. But the foregoing powers of the soul would be maximally subject to reason if this rebellion were totally quelled. Therefore, this would especially belong to human nature and thus the impediment of this rebellion could be totally removed by us.

9. Moreover, it does not suffice for the notion of virtue that vice be avoided, for the perfection of justice consists in what is said in Psalm 33, 15: "Forsake evil and do good." But it is a note of the irascible that it detests evil, as is said in *Of the spirit and soul.* Therefore, virtue can be in the irascible at least.

10. Moreover, in the same book it is said that in reason there is a desire for virtues, but in the irascible a hatred of vice. But the desire for virtue and virtue are in the same power, since a thing desires its own perfection. Therefore, every virtue is in reason and not in the irascible and concupiscible.

11. Moreover, no potency which is only acted upon and does not act can have a habit, since a habit is that whereby one acts when he wishes, as the Commentator says in *On the soul* 3. But the irascible and concupiscible do not act, but are acted upon, because as is said in *Ethics* 3, sense is not the master of any act. Therefore, there cannot be a habit of virtue in the irascible and concupiscible.

12. Moreover, the proper subject is commensurate with the proper passion. But virtue is commensurate with reason and not with the irascible and concupiscible, which are common to the brutes and us. That is why virtue like reason is found only in men. Therefore, every virtue is in reason and none in the irascible and concupiscible.

13. Moreover, the gloss on Romans 7: "The law is good which while it prohibits concupiscence, prohibits every evil." Therefore, all vices pertain to the concupiscible appetite where concupiscence lies. But virtues and vices are in the same subject. Therefore, if not in the irascible, virtues are in the concupiscible at least.

ON THE CONTRARY. 1. There is what the Philosopher says of temperance and fortitude, that they are in irrational parts. But the parts of the irrational, that is, of sense appetite, are the irascible and concupiscible, as is said in *On the soul*. Therefore, there can be virtues in the irascible and concupiscible.

2. Moreover, venial sin is a disposition to mortal sin. But completion and disposition pertain to the same thing. Therefore, since venial sin is in the irascible and concupiscible (for the first movement is the act of sensuality, as is said in the gloss on Romans 8), mortal sin too can be there, and thus virtue too, which is the contrary of mortal sin.

3. Moreover, the middle and extremes belong to the same thing. But virtue is a kind of mean between contrary passions, as courage between fear and boldness, and temperance between too much and too little in things desired. Therefore, since passions of this kind are in the irascible and concupiscible, it seems that virtue too is in them.

RESPONSE. It should be said that everyone is agreed on this question, at least in part, though in part there are conflicting opinions as well. It is conceded by all that there are some virtues in the irascible and concupiscible, such as temperance in the concupiscible and courage in the irascible, but there is this difference. Some distinguish two kinds of irascible and concupiscible, one in the superior, the other in the inferior part of the soul. For they say that the irascible and concupiscible which are in the superior part of the soul, since they pertain to rational nature, can be the subject of virtue, but not those which are in the inferior part and pertain to sensual and brute nature. But this has been discussed in another question, namely, whether in the superior part of the soul two powers can be distinguished, one irascible and the other concupiscible, properly speaking.

But whatever be said of that, so far as the irascible and concupiscible in the inferior appetite are concerned, there must be virtues in them as well, as Aristotle says in *Ethics 3*, and others agree. This is obvious from the following consideration. It has been pointed out that virtue names the fulfillment of a power, and a power looks to act, so virtue is found in a power which is a principle of human action. It is not just any activity found in man or engaged in by a man that is called human, since there are many activities shared by plants, animals, and men, but only that which is proper to him. Unlike these other things, it is proper to man that he have dominion over his acts. Any act over which a man has dominion is properly called a human act, but not those over which he does not have dominion, even though they occur in him, e.g., digesting and growing and the like. Therefore, there can be virtue in that which is a principle of an act over which man has dominion.

Therefore, any act of which man is master is properly a human act, but not those of which he is not, even though they occur in a man, such as digesting, growing, and the like. Therefore, there can be human virtue in that thanks to which man has domain over his acts. But it should be noted that acts of this kind have a threefold principle. One that is the first and commanding mover, thanks to which man has dominion over his acts, and this is reason or will. The other is a moved mover, namely, sense appetite, which is moved by the higher appetite insofar as it obeys it and then by its command moves the external members. Third, there is that which is only moved, namely, the external members.

However, although both the external members and the inferior appetite are moved by the higher part of the soul, this does not happen in the same way. For, in the nature of things, such external members as the hand or foot obey the command of the higher straightaway without any resistance, unless there be some impediment. But the lower appetite has an inclination of its own following on its nature and does not automatically obey the higher appetite. Hence, Aristotle says in the *Politics* that the soul rules the body as a despot would, as a master rules a slave who does not have the capacity to resist the master's command. But reason rules the inferior parts of the soul with a royal and political governance, that is, as kings and princes rule free men who have the right and capacity to resist to some degree the commands of king or prince.

Therefore, there is no need in the external member for anything perfective of the human act, save its natural disposition by which it is fashioned to be moved by reason. But in the inferior appetite, which can resist reason, there is need for something whereby the activity that reason commands be accomplished without resistance. For if the immediate principle of operation is imperfect, the operation must be imperfect, however much perfection is found in the higher principle. Therefore, if the lower appetite is not perfected by a disposition to follow the command of reason, the operation, which is from the lower appetite as from its proper principle, would not be of perfect goodness. For there would be some resistance of sense appetite, and a sadness would result in sense appetite, since it would be moved as it were violently by the higher. This happens in those who have strong desires which they do not, however, follow because of reason's prohibition.

Therefore, when human action must deal with the objects of sense appetite, the good of the operation requires that there be a disposition or perfection in sense appetite by which it easily obeys reason. This is what we call virtue. Therefore, when there is a virtue with respect to that which pertains to the irascible power, such as courage with respect to fear and boldness, or magnanimity with respect to difficult things hoped for, and patience with respect to anger, such virtues are said to be in the irascible as in their subject. But when it is a matter of things which properly pertain to the concupiscible, they are said to be in the concupiscible as in their subject, such as chastity, which is concerned with venereal pleasure, and sobriety and abstinence, which are concerned with the pleasures of food and drink.

Ad 1. It should be said that virtue and mortal sin can be considered as acts or as habits. For the acts of the concupiscible and irascible, considered in themselves, are not mortal sins, but turn into mortal sin when, with reason consenting or moving, they tend to what is contrary to divine law. Some of these acts then, taken as such, cannot be acts of virtue, but only when they concur in following the command of reason. Thus the act of mortal sin and of virtue pertain in a way to the irascible and concupiscible, and that is why the habit of either can be in the irascible and concupiscible. And so in the case in point: Just as the act of virtue consists in this that the irascible and concupiscible follow reason, so the act of sin consists in this, that reason is drawn to follow the inclination of the irascible and concupiscible. That is why sin and the virtues of the irascible and concupiscible are often attributed to reason as to their proximate cause.

Ad 2. It should be said that, as has been pointed out already, the act of virtue cannot be of the irascible and concupiscible alone, apart from reason. Choice, the chief thing in the act of virtue, comes from reason, and, as in any activity, the action of the agent is prior to the passion of the patient. But reason commands the irascible and concupiscible. Therefore, virtue is not said to be in the irascible or concupiscible as if the whole act of virtue or even its chief part were accomplished by them, but insofar as, by the habit of virtue, the ultimate fulfillment of goodness is conferred on the act of virtue, such that the irascible and concupiscible follow the command of reason without difficulty.

Ad 3. It should be said that, supposing that the irascible and concupiscible do not actually remain in the separated soul, they would still remain in it as in their root, for the essence of the soul is the root of the powers. Similarly, virtues which are ascribed to the irascible and concupiscible remain in reason as in their root, for reason is the root of all the virtues, as will be shown later.

Ad 4. It should be said that a certain hierarchy is found in forms. For some forms and powers are totally immersed in matter and their activities are wholly material, as is evident of the forms of elements.

But the intellect is wholly free from matter, so its operation does not involve any sharing in matter. The irascible and are in a midway condition. For the bodily change conjoined to their acts shows that they use a bodily organ, but that they are in some way lifted above matter is shown by this, that they are moved on command and obey reason. So there is virtue in them insofar as they are lifted above matter and obey reason.

Ad 5. It should be said that although the order of reason in which the irascible and concupiscible participate is not something subsistent and cannot be a subject as such, yet it can be the reason why something is a subject.

Ad 6. It should be said that the powers of sense knowledge are naturally prior to reason since reason receives from them, but the appetitive naturally follow the order of reason since the lower appetite naturally obeys the higher, and so it is not similar.

Ad 7. It should be said that the rebellion against reason by the irascible and concupiscible cannot be wholly removed by virtue; since of their very nature the irascible and concupiscible tend to that which is good according to sense, they sometimes resist reason. But this can be brought about by the divine power which is even capable of changing natures. Nevertheless, this rebellion is diminished by virtue insofar as these powers become accustomed to being subject to reason, and thus, they have what pertains to virtue from outside, namely, from the dominion of reason over them. Of themselves they retain something of the movements proper to them which are sometimes contrary to reason.

Ad 8. It should be said that although there is in man the principle of reason, the integrity of human nature requires not only reason, but also the lower powers, and the body too. So it is that left to itself the condition of human nature is such that there is resistance to reason on the part of the lower powers, something which follows on the fact that these lower powers of the soul have their own activities. It is otherwise in the state of innocence and of glory, since reason thanks to its union with God draws strength to contain entirely the lower powers.

Ad 9. It should be said insofar as the detestation of evil is said to pertain to the irascible, it not only implies a turning away from evil but a move by the irascible to destroy evil, much like one who not only flees evil but is moved by anger to extirpate evil. But this is to do something good. Although evil is thus detested, it is not only this that pertains to the irascible and concupiscible, for to pursue an arduous good pertains to the irascible, in which there is not only the motion of wrath and boldness but of hope.

Ad 10. It should be said that those words must be understood by way of adaption and not properly, for in every power of the soul there is a desire for a proper good, so the irascible desires victory as the concupiscible desires pleasure. But because the concupiscible is drawn to something simply or absolutely good for the whole animal, every desire of the good is attributed to it.

Ad 11. It should be said that, although the irascible and concupiscible, considered as such, are acted upon and do not act, however, insofar as in man they participate somewhat in reason they also in a way act and are not wholly acted upon. Hence, in the *Politics* the Philosopher says the reason's dominion over these powers is political, because such powers retain their own activities and do not obey reason completely. The soul's dominion over body is not royal but despotic, because the members of the body instantly obey the soul so far as their activities go.

Ad 12. It should be said that although these powers are found in brutes, in them they do not participate in reason and thus they cannot have moral virtues.

Ad 13. It should be said all evil can be laid to concupiscence as to its ultimate, but not to its proximate, root. All passions take their rise from the concupiscible and irascible, as was shown when we dealt with the emotions. Indeed, the perversity of reason and will most often come about because of the emotions. Or we could say that we understand by concupiscence not only the concupiscible power itself but what is common to all appetitive powers, in each species of which there is to be found something of concupiscence, because of which sin occurs. One cannot otherwise sin than by desiring and seeking.

Article 5

Whether will is the subject of virtue

And it seems that it is.

1. A greater perfection is needed in the commander if he is to command perfectly than in the executor if he is to execute well, because the order to execute comes from the commander. But the will commands the act of virtue, and the irascible and concupiscible obey and execute. Therefore, since virtue exists in the irascible and concupiscible as in a subject, it seems that it should even more so be in the will.

2. It will be said that the will's natural inclination to the good suffices for its rectitude, since we naturally desire the end, so it does not need to be rectified by a superadded habit of virtue. On the contrary: Will does not bear on the ultimate end alone, but also on other ends. But with respect to the desire for other ends the will can act rightly or not rightly. For the good propose for themselves good ends, and the evil evil, as is said in *Ethics* 3: As a person is, so does the end appear to him. Therefore, for rectitude of will there is required that there be in it some habit of virtue that perfects it.

3. Moreover, the soul's knowing power has some natural knowledge, namely, of first principles, yet we have an intellectual virtue with respect to such knowledge, namely, insight (*intellectus*), which is the habit of first principles. So there should be in will a virtue with respect to that to which it is naturally inclined.

4. Moreover, just as there is moral virtue governing the emotions, namely temperance and courage, so there is a virtue governing actions, namely justice. But will acts without emotion while the irascible and concupiscible are with emotion. Therefore, just as there is moral virtue in the irascible and concupiscible, so too is there in the will.

5. Morever, the Philosopher says in *Ethics* 4 that love or friendship involves emotion. But friendship is a matter of choice, and the love that is without passion is an act of will. Therefore, since friendship is a virtue, or not without virtue, as is said in *Ethics* 8, it seems that there is also virtue in will as in a subject.

6. Moreover, charity is the most powerful of the virtues, as the

Apostle proves in 1 Corinthians 13. But only will can be the subject of charity; the concupiscible, which is lower, cannot be its subject since it bears only on sensible goods. Therefore, will is the subject of virtue.

7. Moreover, according to Augustine we are conjoined to God most immediately through will. But that which conjoins us to God is virtue. Therefore, it seems that virtue is in will as in a subject.

8. Moreover, happiness according to Hugh of St. Victor is in the will. But virtues are dispositions to happiness. Therefore, since disposition and perfection are in the same thing, it seems that virtue is in will as in a subject.

9. Moreover, according to Augustine, will is that whereby we either live rightly or sin. But rectitude of life pertains to virtue. Hence, Augustine says that virtue is a good quality of mind, whereby we live rightly. Therefore, virtue is in the will.

10. Moreover, contraries are such as to be in the same subject; but sin is contrary to virtue. Therefore, just as every sin is in the will, as Augustine says, so it seems that every virtue too must be in the will.

11. Moreover, human virtue ought to be in the part of the soul that it proper to man. But will is proper to man, just as reason is, as being closer to reason than are the irascible and concupiscible. Therefore, since the irascible and concupiscible are subject of virtue, it seems that the will should be *a fortiori.*

ON THE CONTRARY. 1. Every virtue is either intellectual or moral, as is clear from what the Philosopher says at the end of *Ethics* 1. But moral virtue has as its subject that which is rational by participation, not essentially. But intellectual virtue has for subject that which is rational essentially. Therefore, since the will can be counted in neither part, since it is not a knowing power, which pertains to the essentially rational, nor does it pertain to the rational by way of participation, it seems that the will can in no way be the subject of virtue.

2. Moreover, several virtues ought not pertain to the same act, but that is what would happen if the will were the subject of virtue because, as has been shown, there are virtues in the irascible and

concupiscible, and since will is related in some way to the acts of those virtues, there would have to be virtues in the will related to those acts. Therefore, it should not be said that the will is the subject of virtue.

RESPONSE. It should be said that a power acquires a complement to its act from the habit of virtue to which it is subject. Hence, a habit of virtue is not needed in order for a power to extend to its proper objects. Virtue orders the power to the good, since virtue is what makes the one having it good and renders his act good. But will has by reason of itself that which other powers have as a result of virtue, since its object is the good. Hence, for the will to tend to the good is like the concupiscible tending to the pleasurable and hearing to sound. Hence, the will is in no need of a habit of virtue in order to be inclined to the good proportioned to it, to which it tends because of what it is, but with respect to the good which transcends what is proportioned to the power, it needs a habit of virtue. Since it is the nature of any appetite to tend to the proper good of the desirer, a good can exceed the proportion of will in two ways.

In one way by reason of the species, in another by reason of the individual. By reason of the species, as when the will is elevated to a good that exceeds the limits of the human good, and by human I mean what a man can do with his own powers. But the divine good is above the human good, and charity raises man's will to that, and so does hope.

By reason of the individual, as when someone seeks the good of another, although the will is not borne beyond the limits of the human good, and thus justice perfects will as do all the virtues which relate to the other, such as liberality and the like. For justice is the good of the other, as the Philosopher says in *Ethics* 5. Thus, there are two virtues in will as in a subject, namely, charity and justice. A sign of this is that these virtues, although they pertain to appetite, are not about emotions, as temperance and courage are, and thus, it is clear that they are not in sense appetite in which the emotions are found, but in rational appetite, that is, will, in which there are no emotions. For every emotion is in the sensitive part of the soul, as is proved in *Physics* 8. But those virtues which concern the emotions, as courage concerns fear and boldness, and temperance desire, must for this reason be in sense appetite. Nor need there be any virtue in the will because of such emotions, because the good of such emotions is according to reason. To which, since it is its proper object, the will is naturally disposed by reason of what it is.

Ad 1. It should be said that the judgment of reason suffices for the will to command, since will naturally seeks the good according to reason, as the concupiscible seeks what is pleasurable to the sense.

Ad 2. It should be said that the natural inclination of will is not only to the ultimate end, but to the good shown to it by reason. For the good as understood is the object of will and to it the will is naturally ordered, as any power is ordered to its own object, so long as it is its proper good, as was said earlier. But one can sin in this regard insofar as the judgment of reason is intercepted by emotion.

Ad 3. It should be said that knowledge comes about through some likeness (species), nor does the power of intellect suffice of itself for knowing unless it receives an intelligible species. That is why in things that we know naturally there must be some habit which also takes its rise from the senses, as is said at the end of the *Posterior Analytics*. But will does not need any species in order to will, so the case is not similar.

Ad 4. It should be said that the virtues which concern emotions are in the lower appetite, nor is any virtue of the higher appetite required for them, for the reason already given.

Ad 5. It should be said that friendship is not a virtue properly speaking, but something following on virtue. For because one is virtuous it follows that he will love those like himself. It is otherwise with charity, which is a friendship with God that lifts man up to that which exceeds the limits of his nature. Hence, charity is in the will, as we said.

Ad 6 & 7. From this the reply to six and seven are obvious, for the virtue joining the will to God is charity.

Ad 8. It should be said that certain dispositions are prerequisites to happiness, such as the acts of the moral virtues by which impediments to happiness are removed, such as disturbance of the mind by passions and external distractions. But there is an act of virtue which when it is complete is essentially happiness, namely, the act of reason or intellect. For contemplative happiness is nothing else than the perfect contemplation of the highest truth; but active happiness is the act of prudence by which a man governs himself and others. But there is something perfective of happiness, namely, pleasure which completes happiness as comeliness does youth, as is said in *Ethics* 10. This pertains to will, and if we are speaking of celestial happiness which is promised to the saints, the will is ordered to it by charity, but if we are speaking of contemplative happiness, the will is ordered to it by a natural desire. Thus, it is clear that not all virtues need be in the will.

Ad 9. It should be said that one lives rightly or sinfully by will which commands all the acts of virtues and vices, although not as eliciting, so it is not necessary that the will be the proximate subject of every virtue.

Ad 10. It should be said that every sin is in the will as in its cause insofar as every sin comes about by consent of the will, but it is not necessary that every sin be in the will as in its subject: Gluttony and dissipation are in the concupiscible, and pride is in the irascible.

Ad 11. It should be said that from will's closeness to reason it happens that will is in harmony with reason just because of what it is, and therefore, there is no need of any habit of virtue besides, as there is with the lower powers, namely, the irascible and concupiscible.

REPLIES TO ARGUMENTS ON THE CONTRARY

Ad 1. It should be said that charity and hope which are in the will are not included in this division of philosophy, for they are another kind of virtue called theological. Justice is included among the moral virtues, for the will like other appetites participates in reason in the sense that it is directed by reason. For although will belongs by nature to the same intellectual part as reason, it is not the same power as reason.

Ad 2. It should be said that with respect to the things to which a virtue of the irascible or concupiscible relates, there need be no virtue in will, for the reason already given.

Article 6
Whether practical intellect is the subject of virtue

It seems that it is not.

1. The Philosopher says in *Ethics* 2 that knowing is of little or no avail for virtue, and he is speaking there of practical knowledge, as is clear from what he adds, that many do not do the things of which they have knowledge: It is the knowledge of practical reason that is ordered to action. Therefore, practical intellect cannot be the subject of virtue.

2. Moreover, without virtue no one can act rightly. But without the perfection of practical intellect, a person can act rightly, since he can be instructed by someone else concerning things to be done. Therefore, the perfection of practical intellect is not a virtue.

3. Moreover, the more one sins, the more he recedes from virtue. But departure from the perfection of practical intellect lessens sin, for ignorance excuses either in part or in full. Therefore, the perfection of practical intellect cannot be a virtue.

4. Moreover, according to Cicero, virtue acts as nature does, but nature's manner of acting is opposed to that of reason, that is, of practical intellect, something clear from *Physics 2,* where the natural is distinguished from the way in which one acts knowingly. Therefore, it would seem that there is no virtue in the practical intellect.

5. Moreover, the good and the true are formally different in their proper notions, but the formal difference of objects diversifies habits. Therefore, since the object of virtue is the good, whereas the perfection of practical intellect is the true, although ordered to action, it seems that the perfection of practical intellect is not virtue.

6. Moreover, according to Aristotle in *Ethics* 2, virtue is a voluntary habit, but the habits of practical intellect differ from those of will or the appetitive part. Therefore, the habits which are in practical intellect are not virtues. Consequently, the practical intellect is not the subject of virtue.

ON THE CONTRARY. 1. Prudence is one of the four principal virtues, but its subject is practical intellect. Therefore, practical intellect can be the subject of virtue.

2. Moreover, human virtue has a human power for its subject. But intellect is more of a human power than are the irascible and concupiscible, since that which is something essentially is greater than that which is such only by participation. Therefore, the practical intellect is the subject of human virtue.

3. Moreover, that for the sake of which something is takes precedence, but in the affective part virtue is for the sake of reason, since in order that the affective power might obey reason a virtue is established in it. All the more reason, then, why there should be a virtue in practical reason.

RESPONSE. It should be said that there is this difference between natural and rational virtue that the former is determined to one, whereas the latter is ordered to many things. Both animal and rational appetites are inclined to what they desire by means of a preexisting cognition. As for natural appetite, it tends to its end without any pre-existent knowledge, as the heavy inclines to the center. Because the known good is the object of animal and rational appetites, where this good is always the same, there can be a natural inclination in appetite and a natural judgment in the cognitive power, as happens in beasts which have few activities because of the weakness of the active power which extends to few. In all things of the same species there is the same unchanging good. Hence, they have a natural inclination to it and a natural judgment in the cognitive power with respect to that uniform good. From this natural judgment and desire it comes about that all swallows builds their nests in the same way and all spiders spin a web the same way, and so it is with all beasts. But man has many and different activities because of the nobility of his active principle, the soul, whose power extends in a way to an infinity of things. Therefore, the natural desire of the good does not suffice for man, or the natural judgment for acting well, unless they be further determined and perfected.

A man is inclined by natural appetite to seek his proper good, but since this varies in many ways and because man's good consists of many things, there could not be a natural appetite in man for this determinate good given all the conditions needed if it is to be good for him, since this varies widely according to the condition of persons, times, and places and the like. For the same reason the natural judgment, which is uniform, does not suffice for the pursuit of a good of this kind. So it is that a man must by reason, which compares different things, discover and discern his proper good, determined with respect to all its conditions insofar as it sought here and now.

With respect to doing, reason without a perfecting habit is like speculative reason without the habit of science when it judges the conclusion of some science, something it can do only imperfectly and with difficulty. Thus it is that speculative reason needs to be perfected by the habit of science in order to judge the objects pertaining to that science; so too practical reason is perfected by a habit in order that it might rightly judge the human good with respect to all the things that must be done. This virtue is called prudence and its subject is practical reason; it is perfective of the moral virtues in the appetitive part, all of which incline appetite to some type of human good, as justice gives an inclination to the good of equality in things pertaining to common life, temperance to the good which is the restraint of desire, and so with the other virtues, every one of which is exercised in many ways and not uniformly in every case. That is why prudence of judgment is needed in order that the right mode be established.

From this the rectitude and completion of goodness in all other virtues comes; hence, the Philosopher says that the mean in moral virtue is determined by right reason. Because all the habits of the appetitive part take the note of virtue from this rectitude and completion of goodness, virtue is the cause of all the virtues of the appetitive part, which are called moral insofar as they are virtues. Moreover, Gregory in the *Morals on Job 22* says that the other virtues can be virtues only insofar as they do prudently what they seek.

Ad 1. It should be said that the Philosopher is speaking there of practical science, and prudence implies more than practical science. Practical science makes a universal judgment of things to be done, for example, fornication is evil, theft ought not be committed, and the like. This knowledge can be present yet reason's judgment concerning the particular act be intercepted with the result that one does not judge correctly. That is why moral science is said to avail little for the acquisition of virtue, because even when it is had a man can sin against virtue. It is the task of prudence to judge correctly concerning singular things to be done, to be done now, a judgment that is indeed corrupted by any sin. Therefore, while prudence remains, a man does not sin. Hence, it avails not a little but much for virtue, indeed it causes virtue, as has been said.

Ad 2. It should be said that a man can take general advice from another concerning what is to be done, but that he rightly follow it in action against all passions can only result from the rectitude of prudence without which virtue simply would not be.

Ad 3. It should be said that the ignorance which is the opposite of prudence is ignorance of choice according to which every evil is due to the ignorance which follows on the interception of reason's judgment by the inclination of appetite. And this is no excuse for sin, since it constitutes it, but the ignorance which is opposed to practical science excuses or diminishes sin.

Ad 4. It should be said that Cicero's remark is to be understood as applying to the inclination of appetite tending to some general good, such as acting courageously and the like. But if this inclination is not directed by the judgment of reason, it is frequently led astray and so much the more as it is more vehement, as the Philosopher says in *Ethics* 6 of the blind man who is the more injured by hitting the wall the faster he runs.

Ad 5. It should be said that the good and true are objects of different parts of the soul, namely, of the intellective and the appetitive, which two are so related that both act on the act of the other, as will wishes the intellect to understand and intellect understands the will to will. Therefore, these two, good and true, include one another, since the good is a kind of truth, insofar as it is grasped by intellect when intellect understands the will to be willing the good or even insofar as it understands that something is good. So too the true is a good of intellect which thus falls to the will insofar as a man wills to understand the true. Nevertheless, the truth of the practical intellect is the good, which is the end of action, for good does not move appetite save insofar as it is understood. Therefore, nothing prevents there being a virtue in practical intellect.

Ad 6. It should be said that the Philosopher defines moral virtue in *Ethics* 2 and intellectual virtue in *Ethics* 6. The virtue that is in practical intellect is not moral but intellectual, since the Philosopher numbers prudence among the intellectual virtues, as is evident in *Ethics* 2.

Article 7

Are there virtues of the speculative intellect?

It seems that there are not.

1. Every virtue is ordered to action, since virtue is what renders action good. But the speculative intellect is not ordered to action, for it says nothing of imitating or fleeing, as is clear from *On the soul* 3. Therefore, there can be no virtue of the speculative intellect.

2. Moreover, virtue is what makes the one having it good, as is said in *Ethics* 2. But a habit of speculative intellect does not make the one having it good; one is not called a good man because he possesses science. Therefore, the habits which are found in the speculative intellect are not virtues.

3. Moreover, the speculative intellect is chiefly perfected by the habit of science, but science is not a virtue, as is clear from the fact that it is distinguished from the virtues. For a habit or disposition is said to be in the first species of quality, and habit is predicated of science and virtue. Therefore, there is no virtue of the speculative intellect.

4. Moreover, every virtue is ordered to something, namely, happiness which is the end of virtue. But the speculative intellect is not ordered to anything; speculative sciences are not sought for the sake of utility, but for themselves, as is said in *Metaphysics* 1. Therefore, there cannot be a virtue in the speculative intellect.

5. Moreover, the act of virtue is meritorious. But understanding does not suffice for merit, indeed one who knows the good and does not do it sins, as is said in James 4, 17. Therefore, there is no virtue of speculative intellect.

ON THE CONTRARY. 1. Faith is in the speculative intellect, since its object is the First Truth. But faith is a virtue. Therefore, the speculative intellect can be the subject of virtue.

2. Moreover, the true and good are equally noble, for they include one another, for the true is a kind of good and the good is a kind of truth, and both are common to every being. Therefore, if

there can be virtue in the will, whose object is the good, there can be virtue in speculative intellect, whose object is the true.

RESPONSE. It should be said that virtue in anything is said with respect to the good, because, as the Philosopher says, any virtue makes the one having it good and renders his action good. For example, the virtue of the horse makes the horse good and makes him run well and sit a rider well, and these are the functions of a horse. To the degree then that a habit has the note of virtue, it is ordered to the good. But this occurs in two ways, formally and materially.

Formally, when a habit is ordered to the good as good; materially when it is ordered to something that is good but not under the note of goodness. Good under the note of goodness is the object of the appetitive part alone, for good is that which all things seek. Therefore, those habits which are either in the appetitive part or depend upon it are formally ordered to the good and are called virtues in the strongest sense. Habits which are not in the appetitive part nor depend upon it can be materially ordered to that which is good although not formally under the note of goodness, hence they can in some way be called virtues, though not so properly as the first habits. But it should be noted that the intellect, both speculative and practical, can be perfected by a habit in two ways.

In one way absolutely and as such, insofar as it precedes will as moving it; in another way insofar as it follows will which elicits its act on command, because, as has been said, these two powers, intellect and will, involve one another. Therefore, the habits which are in practical or speculative intellect in the first way can be called virtues in a way, though not according to the full sense of the term, and so it is with understanding, science, and wisdom in the speculative intellect, and art in the practical intellect. For one is said to be knowing or understanding insofar as his intellect is perfected with respect to knowing the truth, which indeed is the good of intellect. And although the true can be willed, insofar as a man wishes to understand the truth, it is not in this respect that the foregoing habits perfect.

For a man is not made willing to consider the truth by the fact that he has science: He is only capable of it. Hence, the very consideration of the true is not science as it is willed, but insofar as it tends directly to its object. And similarly in the case of art in the practical intellect, which is why art does not perfect a man in such a way that he wills to act according to the art, but only that he should know and be capable. But habits which are in speculative or practical intellect insofar as intellect follows will more truly have the note of virtue, since by them a man is made not only capable or cognizant of acting well, but willing. This can be seen in the case of faith and prudence, though differently. Faith perfects the speculative intellect insofar as it is commanded by will, which is clear from its act, for a man does not give intellectual assent to what is above human reason unless he wills to; as Augustine says: "No man can believe unless he is willing."

Just as faith is in the speculative intellect following the command of will, so temperance is in the concupiscible insofar as it is subject to the command of reason. Hence, in believing will commands intellect, not only with respect to bringing off the act, but also with respect to the determination of its object, since intellect assents to a definite belief on the will's command, just as in the determination of the mean by reason the concupiscible tends because of temperance. But prudence is in practical intellect or reason, as has been said, and will determines only the end of prudence, not its object: For prudence seeks its object presupposing the will for the good end, inquiring into ways whereby this good can be achieved and retained.

Thus it is clear that habits of intellect are related to will in different ways, for some depend on will only for their use, and this is incidental to them. Use depends on will in one way and on such habits as science and wisdom and art in another. These habits do not perfect a man in such a way that he chooses to use them well, but give him only the capacity. But there is an intellectual habit which receives its principle or starting point from will, for in action the end is the starting point. This is how it is with prudence. There is another intellectual habit which receives its determinate object from the will, and this is faith.

Now all these habits can be called virtues but not in the same sense. These last two more perfectly and properly fulfill the definition of virtue, although from this it does not follow that they are more noble or more perfect habits.

Ad 1. It should be said that a habit of speculative intellect is ordered to its proper act which makes it perfect, that is, to the consideration of truth, but it is not ordered to some external action as to an end: Its end lies in its proper act. But practical intellect is ordered to an external action as to its end, for the consideration of what ought to be done or made pertains to practical intellect for the sake of acting or doing. Thus, the habit of speculative intellect makes its act good in a more noble way than does the habit of practical intellect, the former as an end, the latter as for an end, even though the habit of practical intellect, insofar as it orders to the good as good, and presupposes the will, is more properly called virtue.

Ad 2. It should be said that a man is not said to be simply good when he is only partially good but only when he is good as a whole, which comes about by the goodness of will. The will commands the acts of all human powers, because every act is the good of its power. Thus, a man will be called simply good when he has a good will. But he who has goodness with respect to some power, not presupposing a good will, is called good insofar as he has good sight or hearing or is said to see and hear well. It is clear from this that a man is not said to be absolutely good just because he knows; he is only said to think well, and the same is true with respect to art and other like habits.

Ad 3. It should be said that science is distinguished from moral virtue yet is an intellectual virtue; it is also distinguished from virtue in the most proper sense, for it is not that kind of virtue, as has been said.

Ad 4. It should be said that the speculative intellect is not ordered to something outside itself, but it is ordered to its own act as to an end. Ultimate, that is, contemplative, happiness consists in its activity. Hence, the acts of speculative intellect are closer to ultimate happiness by way of similarity than the habits of practical intellect, though the habits of practical intellect are perhaps closer by way of preparation or merit.

Ad 5. It should be said that by the act of such a habit as science a man can merit insofar as it is commanded by will without which there is no merit. However, science does not perfect intellect in that way, as has been said. A man is not made willing to use it from the fact that he has knowledge, but only capable. Therefore, a bad will is not opposed to science or art as it is to prudence, faith, or temperance. Hence, the Philosopher says that he who sins voluntarily in things to be done is less prudent, though it is the opposite in science and art: The grammarian who deliberately commits a solecism is no less a grammarian.

Article 8
Do we have any natural virtues?

It seems that we do.

1. St. John Damascene said in Book Three, Chapter 14, "Virtues are natural and are in us naturally and equally."

2. Moreover, the gloss on Matthew 4, 23, says: He teaches natural justice, namely, chastity, justice, humility, virtues a man has naturally.

3. Moreover, it is said in Romans 2, 14, that men who have not the law naturally do what is of the law. But law commands the act of virtue. Therefore, men naturally perform the acts of virtue, and so it seems that virtue is from nature.

4. Moreover, Anthony says in a sermon to monks, "If will changed nature, it would be perversity; if the condition is preserved, it is virtue." And in the same sermon he says that natural adornment suffices for a man. But this would not be if the virtues were not natural. Therefore, the virtues are natural.

5. Moreover, Cicero says that elevation of soul is ours by nature, but this seems to refer to magnanimity. Therefore, magnanimity is in us naturally and for the same reason the other virtues.

6. Moreover, to do the work of virtue nothing is needed but being capable of the good, to will it and to know it. But the notion of good is in us naturally, as Augustine says in *On free will* 2. But to will the good is natural to man, as Augustine says when commenting literally on Genesis. "To be capable of the good is in man naturally, since the will has dominion over his acts. Therefore, nature suffices for the work of virtue. Therefore, virtue is natural to man, with respect to its beginning over his acts.

7. But it might be said that virtue is natural to man as to its beginning, but its perfection is not from nature. On the contrary, there is what Damascene says in Book Three, Chapter 14: "Remaining in that which is according to nature, we are in virtue; but falling away from that which is according to nature, from virtue, we arrive at that which is against nature and we are in evil." From which it is clear that to turn away from evil is according to nature, but this is the mark of perfect virtue. There the perfection of virtue too is from nature.

8. Moreover, virtue, since it is a form, is something simple, lacking parts. Therefore, if it is according to nature in some part, it is totally from nature.

9. Moreover, man is more worthy and perfect that irrational creatures, but in what pertains to their perfection nature is sufficient for such creatures. Therefore, since the virtues are perfections of man, it seems that they are in man by nature.

10. But it will be said that this cannot be because man's perfection lies in many and diverse things whereas nature is ordered to one. On the contrary. The inclination of virtue like that of nature is to one. For Cicero says that virtue is a habit after the manner of nature, in agreement with reason. Therefore nothing prevents virtues from being in man from nature.

11. Moreover, virtue consists in the mean, but the mean is determined to one. Therefore, nothing prevents nature from inclining to the same thing as virtue.

12. Moreover, sin is the privation of mode, species, and order. But sin is the privation of virtue. Therefore, virtue consists in mode, species, and order. But these three are natural to man. Therefore, virtue is natural to man.

13. Moreover, the appetitive part of the soul follows the cognitive part, but in the cognitive part there is a certain natural habit, namely, the understanding of principles. Therefore, there must be a natural habit in the appetitive and affective part of the soul which is the subject of virtue. Therefore, there seems to be some virtue that is natural.

14. Moreover, the natural is that whose principle is within, as to be borne upward is natural to fire, because the principle of this motion is in that which is moved. But the principle of virtue is in man. Therefore, virtue is natural to man.

15. Moreover, that whose seed is natural is itself natural, but the seed of virtue is natural, for a gloss on Hebrews 1 says that God willed to sow in every soul the beginnings of wisdom and understanding. It seems, therefore, that the virtues are natural.

16. Moreover, contraries are of the same genus, but virtue is contrary to evil. But evil is natural, for it is said in Wisdom 12, 10, "and

their malice natural" and Ephesians 2, 3, "and were by nature children of the wrath." Therefore, it seems that virtue is natural.

17. Moreover, it is natural for the lower powers to be subject to reason, for the Philosopher says in *On the soul* 3 that the appetite of the higher part, which is reason, moves the lower, which is of the sensitive part, as the higher sphere moves the lower. But moral virtue consists in this, that the lower powers are subject to reason. Therefore, such virtues are natural.

18. Moreover, in order for a motion to be natural it suffices that there be a natural aptitude of the inner passive principle. This is how the generation of simple bodies is said to be natural; the active power of the celestial bodies is not nature, but intellect, so that the principle of generation of simple bodies is extrinsic to them. But in man there is a natural aptitude for virtue. Aristotle says in *Ethics 2*: We receive the innate from nature but the perfected from practice. It seems, then, that virtue is natural.

19. Moreover, that which is in a man from birth is natural, but according to the Philosopher in *Ethics* 6 some seem from birth to be courageous and temperate and disposed to other virtues. And Job 31, 18, says, "For from my infancy mercy grew up with me and it came out with me from my mother's womb." Therefore, virtues are natural to man.

20. Moreover, nature does not fail in what is necessary, but virtues are necessary for a man given the end to which he is ordered, namely, happiness, which is the act of perfect virtue. Therefore, a man has virtues from nature.

ON THE CONTRARY. 1. The natural is not removed by sin. Hence Dionysius says that what was given by nature survives even in the devils. But virtues are taken away by sin. Therefore, they are not natural.

2. Moreover, we neither acquire nor lose that which is in us naturally and is from nature. But we can acquire and lose what pertains to virtue. Therefore, the virtues are not natural.

3. Moreover, what is naturally in us is in everyone. But the virtues

are not common to all, because in some are found vices contrary to virtue.

4. Moreover, we neither gain nor lose merit because of what is natural in us. But we merit by the virtues as we lost merit by vices. Therefore, the virtues and vices are not natural.

RESPONSE. It should be said that there is a division of opinion concerning the acquisition of sciences and virtues like that concerning the production of natural forms.

For there were those who held that forms actually pre-exist in matter, though latently, and then are brought from a hidden to a manifest state by the natural agent. This was the view of Anaxagoras, who held that everything is in everything, with the result that anything can be generated from anything.

Others said that forms are totally from without, whether by participation in Ideas, as Plato held, or from the agent intellect, as Avicenna thought, and that natural agents only dispose matter for form.

A third and middle way is that of Aristotle who held that forms pre-exist potentially in matter and are brought to act by an external natural agent.

Similarly, in the case of sciences and virtues, some held that sciences and virtues are in us by nature and that by effort it is only impediments to science and virtue that are removed. Plato seems to have held this when he said that sciences and virtues are caused in us by participation in separated forms, but the soul was impeded from using them because of its union with the body, an impediment that must be removed by pursuit of the sciences and the exercise of the virtues. But others said that the sciences and virtues are in us by the influence of the agent intellect, to whose influence a man is disposed by study and exercise. Third is the middle opinion, that sciences and virtues are in us as an aptitude from nature, but their perfection is not in us from nature.

This view is best because just as with natural forms it does not take away the power of natural agents, so it preserves their efficacy with respect to the acquisition of science and virtue by study and exercise. However, it should be noted that the aptitude for perfection and for form can be in a subject in two ways. In one way according to passive potency alone, as in the matter of air there is an aptitude for the form of fire; in another way, according to both active and passive potency, as in the curable body there is an aptitude for health because the body is susceptible of health. It is in this way that there is in man a natural aptitude for virtue, partly indeed due to the nature of species, insofar as the aptitude for virtue is common to all men, and partly due to the nature of the individual, insofar as some are more apt than others for virtue.

For evidence of this, notice that there are three ways in which a man can be a subject of virtue, as is clear from what has already been said; namely, intellect, will, and the lower appetite, which is divided into the concupiscible and irascible. In each of them the manner of susceptibility to virtue and the active principle of virtue must be considered. For it is obvious that in the intellective part there is the possible intellect, which is in potency to all intelligibles, in the knowledge of which intellectual virtue consists, and the agent intellect, in whose light things come to be actually intelligible, some of which a man naturally knows from the outset without study and inquiry, first principles, that is, not only speculative, such as every whole is greater than its part and the like, but also in the practical order, such as evil is to be avoided and the like. These naturally known things are the principles of all subsequent speculative or practical knowledge which is acquired by study.

So too with will it is obvious that there is a natural active principle, for the will is naturally inclined to the ultimate end, and where it is a matter of action the end has the note of a natural principle. Therefore, the inclination of will is an active natural principle with respect to every disposition acquired by the affective part through exercise. But it is clear that the will itself, insofar as it is a power related to many, is susceptible of an habitual inclination to this or that with regard to the means to the end. The concupiscible and irascible naturally heed reason and hence have a natural receptivity to virtue, which is brought to perfection in them insofar as they are disposed to follow the good of reason.

All the foregoing beginnings of virtue follow on the nature of the human species and hence are common to all. But there is another beginning of virtue which follows on individual nature, insofar as a man, by natural makeup or celestial influence, is inclined to the act of a given virtue. This inclination is a kind of beginning of virtue but is not perfected virtue, because for perfected virtue the governance of reason is needed, which is why the definition of virtue states that it is elective of the mean according to right reason. For if someone should follow such an inclination without the discernment of reason, he would frequently sin. Just as this beginning of virtue without the work of reason cannot have the perfect note of virtue, no more can any of the other beginnings of virtue mentioned. For one moves to the specific from universal principles by rational inquiry, and it is by the office of reason too that a man is led from desire of the ultimate end to the things which are appropriate to that end. In commanding the irascible and concupiscible, reason causes them to be subject to itself. So it is clear that for the consummation of virtue the work of reason is required, whether the virtue be in intellect or will or in the irascible or concupiscible. This is the consummation, that the beginning of virtue in the higher part is ordered to the virtue of the lower part, just as a man is made apt for the virtue that is in the will by the beginning of virtue that is in the will, and by that which is in intellect. But the virtue which is in the irascible and concupiscible [is brought to consummation] by the beginnings of virtue in them, and by that which is in the higher, but not vice versa.

Hence, it is manifest that reason, which is higher, works for the completion of every virtue. Both reason and nature are operative principles but they differ, as is clear in *Physics* 2, because the rational power relates to opposites whereas nature is ordered to one. Obviously then the perfection of virtue is from reason, not nature.

Ad 1. It should be said that virtues are called natural because of the natural beginnings of virtue in a man, not because of their perfection.

Ad 2, 3, 4, 5, and 6. The same answer applies to all these.

Ad 6. It should be said that the ability to be good is in us from nature simply speaking in that the powers are natural; but to will and to know are in us by nature in a manner of speaking, namely, according to some general beginning, but this does not suffice for virtue. For good action, which is the effect of virtue, requires that a man promptly and for the most part infallibly attain the good, which no one can do without the habit of virtue. Clearly someone may know generally how to make a work of art, for example to argue, to saw, or to make something, but to do so readily and without error, he has need of art, and it is the same with virtue.

Ad 7. It should be said that for man to turn away from evil is in a way natural, but to do this promptly and infallibly the habit of virtue is needed.

Ad 8. It should be said that virtue is not said to be partly from nature because some part of it is from nature and another not, but because it is from nature according to an imperfect way of being, namely, according to potency and aptitude.

Ad 9. It should be said that God is of himself perfected in goodness; hence, there is no way in which he needs to pursue goodness. The higher substances close to him need little from him in order to achieve the perfection of goodness. But man, who is more remote, needs many things for the pursuit of perfect goodness, because he is capable of happiness. Creatures who are not capable of happiness need fewer things than a man does. Hence, man is more worthy than they, even though he needs more things, just as one who can acquire perfect health by much exercise is better disposed than another who can achieve only a little even though by slight exercise.

Ad 10. It should be said that there can be a natural inclination with respect to the object of one virtue but not with respect to all because the natural disposition which inclines to one virtue inclines to the opposite of another virtue. For example, one naturally disposed to courage, which is the pursuit of the arduous, is less disposed to patience, which consists in restraining the passions of the irascible. Thus we see that animals naturally inclined to the act of one virtue are inclined to a vice contrary to another virtue, as the lion who is bold is also naturally cruel. Such natural inclinations to this or that virtue suffice for animals who are incapable of achieving the perfect good according to virtue but pursue some limited good. But men are made to achieve the perfect good according to virtue and must therefore have an inclination to all the acts of virtue, which, since it cannot be from nature, must come from reason, in which are found the seeds of all the virtues.

Ad 11. It should be said that the mean of virtue is not determined by nature as is the middle of the earth toward which heavy things tend. The mean of virtue must be determined by right reason, as is said in *Ethics* 2, because what is enough for one is too little or too much for another.

Ad 12. It should be said that mode, species, and order constitute any good, as Augustine says in *On the nature of good* 2. Hence, mode, species, and order, in which the good of nature consists, are naturally present in man nor are they taken away by sin. Sin can be called the deprivation of mode, species, and order insofar as the good of virtue consists of these.

Ad 13. It should be said that the will does not produce its act through some species informing it, as the possible intellect does. Therefore, no natural habit for a natural desire is needed in the will, and all the less so because the will is moved by the natural habit of intellect insofar as the known good is the object of will.

Ad 14. It should be said that although the principle of virtue, namely, reason, is within man, this principle does not work in the mode of nature, and that is why what comes from it is not called natural.

Ad 15. The same response suffices for 15.

Ad 16. It should be said that their malice was natural insofar as it was due to custom, since custom is a second nature. But we were by nature the sons of wrath because of original sin, which is a sin of nature.

Ad 17. It should be said that it is natural that the lower powers be subject to reason, but not that they be subject to it according to a habit.

Ad 18. It should be said that motion is said to be natural because of the natural aptitude of the moveable when the mover moves to one determinate thing in the manner of nature, as do the generator of the elements and the mover of the heavenly bodies. But that is not how it is in the case in point, so the argument does not work.

Ad 19. It should be said that the natural inclination to virtue, thanks to which some almost from birth are brave and temperate, does not suffice for perfect virtue, as has been said.

Ad 20. It should be said that nature does not fail man in necessary things, for although it does not provide everything that is necessary for him, it enables him to acquire all necessary things by means of reason and the powers that obey it.

Article 9
Are virtues acquired by acts?

And it seems that they are not.

1. Augustine calls virtue a good quality of mind whereby one acts rightly, which one never uses badly, and which God brings about in us without us. But that which comes about by our acts is not brought about in us by God. Therefore, virtue is not caused by our acts.

2. Moreover, Augustine says that the life of all infidels is sin and that there is no good apart from the supreme good; where knowledge of the truth is lacking, the virtue of even the best is false. From which it follows that virtue cannot be without faith. But faith is not from our doing, but from grace, as is clear in Ephesians 2, 18, "For by grace you have been saved through faith; and that not from yourselves, for it is the gift of God, not as the outcome of works, lest anyone may boast." Therefore, virtue cannot be caused by our acts.

3. Moreover, Bernard says that he labors in vain for virtue who does not know he must hope for it from the Lord. But what one hopes to obtain from God is not caused by our acts. Therefore, virtue is not caused by our acts.

4. Moreover, continence is less than virtue, as is clear from the Philosopher in *Ethics* 7. But we only have continence as a divine gift, for it is said in Wisdom 8, 21, "I know that I cannot be continent unless God grants it." So much the less are we capable of acquiring virtue by our acts, but it must come solely as the gift of God.

5. Moreover, Augustine says that man cannot avoid sin without grace. But sin is avoided by virtue, since a man cannot simultaneously be vicious and virtuous. Therefore, virtue cannot be without grace and thus is not acquired by acts.

6. Moreover, it is through virtue that we come to happiness, for happiness is the reward of virtue, as the Philosopher says in *Ethics* 1. Therefore, if virtue were acquired by our acts, by our acts without grace we could attain life eternal, which is man's ultimate happiness, but that goes against the Apostle in Romans 6, 23, "The gift of God is life everlasting."

7. Moreover, Augustine in *On free will* counts virtue among the

greatest goods because no one uses virtue badly. But the greatest goods are from God, according to James 1, 17, "Every good gift and every perfect gift is from above, coming down from the Father of Lights." Therefore, it seems that virtue is only in us as a gift of God.

8. Moreover, as Augustine says in *On free will* 3, nothing can form itself. But virtue is a kind of form of the soul. Therefore, a man cannot cause virtue in himself by his acts.

9. Moreover, just as from the outset intellect is in essential potency to knowledge, so the affective power is to virtue. But the intellect existing in a state of essential potency needs an external mover, namely, a teacher in order that it might actually know. Similarly therefore, in order for a man to acquire virtue he needs an external agent, and thus his own acts do not suffice.

10. Moreover, acquisition comes about by receiving. But action does not come about by receiving but rather by a sending forth or emergence of action from the agent. Therefore, we do not acquire virtues by the fact that we do things.

11. Moreover, if virtue were acquired by us by our acts, it would be acquired by either one or many. But not by one, since no one is made learned by one act, as is said in *Ethics* 2. Similarly too not by many, because many acts, since they are not simultaneous, cannot together bring about a single effect. Therefore, it seems that there is no way in which virtue could be caused in us by our acts.

12. Moreover, Avicenna says that virtue is the power essentially attributed to things for performing their works. But that which is essentially attributed to a thing is not caused by its act. Therefore, virtue is not caused by the act of the one having virtue.

13. Moreover, if virtue were caused by our acts, this would be either by virtuous or by vicious acts. But not by vicious acts, since they destroy virtue; similarly not by virtuous acts, because they presuppose virtue. Therefore, there is no way that virtue is caused in us by our acts.

14. If it should be said that virtue is caused by imperfect virtuous acts, on the contrary: Nothing acts beyond its species. Therefore, if the acts preceding virtue are imperfect, it seems that they cannot cause perfect virtue.

15. Moreover, virtue is the utmost of a power, as is said in *On the heavens* 1. But a power is natural. Therefore, virtue is natural and not acquired by works.

16. Moreover, virtue is that which makes the one having it good, as is said in *Ethics* 2. But a man is good according to his nature. Therefore, a man's virtue is his from nature and is not acquired by acts.

17. Moreover, a new habit is not acquired by the frequency of a natural act.

18. Moreover, a thing has existence through its form, but grace is the form of the virtues, for without grace the virtues are said to be unformed. Therefore, virtues are from grace and not from acts.

19. Moreover, according to the Apostle [in] 2 Corinthians 12, 9, "strength is made perfect in weakness." But weakness is more of a passion than an act. Therefore, virtue is caused from passion rather than by acts.

20. Moreover, since virtue is a quality, the change brought about by virtue seems to be an alteration, for alteration is change of quality. But alteration is only a passion in the sensitive part of the soul, as is evident from the Philosopher in *Physics* 7. Therefore, if virtue were acquired by our acts by way of some passion and alteration, it would follow that virtue is in the sensitive part. Which conflicts with Augustine who calls it a good quality of mind.

21. Moreover, a person chooses correctly concerning the end thanks to virtue, as is said in *Ethics* 10, but to do this does not seem to be in our power because as one is, so does the end appear to him, as is said in *Ethics* 3, and this is due to natural make-up or the influence of the heavenly bodies. Therefore, it is not in our power to acquire virtues, and they cannot accordingly be caused by our acts.

22. Moreover, we do not become accustomed or unaccustomed with regard to natural things. But in some men there are natural dispositions to some vices, as in others to virtue. Therefore, such inclinations to virtue cannot be wholly taken away by the accustoming due to acts. Thus, while they remain, virtue cannot be in us. Therefore, the virtues cannot be acquired by us through acting.

ON THE CONTRARY. 1. Dionysius says the good is more virtuous than evil, but habits of vice are caused in us by bad acts. Therefore, the habit of virtue is caused in us by good acts.

2. Moreover, according to the Philosopher in *Ethics* 2, activities cause us to be skilled. But this is through virtue. Therefore, virtue is caused in us by acts.

3. Moreover, generation and corruption take place between contraries. But virtue is corrupted by bad acts. Therefore, it is generated by good acts.

RESPONSE. It should be said that since virtue is the utmost of a power, that toward which any power tends in acting, which is that the activity be good, it is manifest that the virtue of anything is that by which it produces its good activity, since anything is for the sake of its activity. A thing is good insofar as it is well related to its end. Thus, a thing must be good and act well because of its own virtue. But the proper good of a thing differs from the proper good of another, different perfections relating to different perfectible things, which is why the good of man is different from the good of a horse or the good of a rock.

But the good of man varies according to different ways of considering him. For there is not the same good of a man as such and as citizen, for the former is the perfection of reason in the knowledge of truth and that the lower powers be regulated by the rule of reason: A man is a man because he is rational. But a man's good insofar as he is a citizen is that he be ordered in all things according to the city, which is why the Philosopher says in *Politics* 3 that the virtue of man as a good man is not the same as the virtue of man as good citizen. But man is not only a citizen of the earthly city, but is also a participant in the heavenly city of Jerusalem whose ruler is the Lord and whose citizens are the angels and all the saints, whether they reign in glory and are at rest in the heaven or are still pilgrims on earth, according to what the Apostle says Ephesians 2, 19, "[Y]ou are citizens with the saints and members of God's household."

A man's nature does not suffice for him to be a participant of this city; he must be elevated by the grace of God. For it is manifest that the virtues that are man's as a participant in this city cannot be acquired by him through his natural powers; hence they are not caused by our acts but are infused in us as a divine gift. But the virtues of a man as man, insofar as he is a citizen of the earthly city, do not exceed the capacity of human nature; hence, a man can acquire them through his natural capacities, by his own acts. This is clear from the fact that everyone has a natural aptitude to some perfection, and if this aptitude is only due to a passive principle, he can acquire it, not by his own act but rather by the act of some external agent, as air receives light from the sun. But if he has a natural aptitude to a perfection due to both an active and passive principle, then he can arrive at it by his own act, as the body of a sick man has a natural aptitude for health. The subject is naturally receptive to health on account of the natural power in him to heal, so even without the action of an external agent, the sick are sometimes made well. But it was shown in the preceding article that man's natural aptitude for virtue is due to active and passive principles, which is clear from the very order of the powers. For in the intellective part there is the quasi-passive power of the possible intellect which is brought to perfection by the agent intellect. But the actualized intellect moves the will, for the known good is the end that moves appetite. But will as moved by reason is so fashioned that it moves the sensitive appetite, namely, the irascible and concupiscible, which are so fashioned as to obey reason. Hence, it is also manifest that any virtue causing good operation in a man has its proper act in man, who by his own action can actualize it, whether it be in intellect, in will or in the irascible and concupiscible.

The virtue of the part does not become actual in the same way as does the virtue of the appetitive part. The action of intellect, or of any other cognitive power, assimilates it to what is known: Intellectual virtue is generated in the intellect when the understood species comes to be in it either actually or habitually thanks to the agent intellect. But the action of the appetitive power inclines us toward the desirable. Hence, in order for virtue to come to be in the appetitive part, it must acquire an inclination to something determinate.

Notice should be taken of the fact that the inclinations of natural things follow their forms, which is why they are ordered to one thing following the demands of the form, and as long as it remains, this inclination cannot be taken from them nor can they be urged toward the opposite. For this reason natural things do not become accustomed or unaccustomed. No matter how often a stone is tossed in the air it will never grow accustomed to height but will always fall. But that which is indifferent in object has no form thanks to which it is inclined determinately; only by its proper mover is it determined to some one thing. Moreover, its being so determined in a way disposes it to the same thing, such that when it is often inclined it is determined to the same effect by its proper agent and a definite inclination is strengthened in it. This superimposed disposition is like a form tending to one in the manner of nature. That is why it is said that custom is a second nature.

It is because the appetitive power is indifferent that it does not tend to one object unless it is determined to do so by reason. When reason repeatedly inclines the appetitive power to some one thing, a disposition is implanted in it by which it is inclined to the thing to which it has become accustomed. It is this implanted disposition that is the habit of virtue. Rightly considered, therefore, the virtue of the appetitive part is nothing other than a disposition or form which is sealed and impressed on it by reason. Because of this, no matter how strong a disposition to something there may be in the appetitive power, it will only be a virtue if it is the result of reason. That is why reason is put into the definition of virtue. Aristotle says in *Ethics 2* virtue is a habit of choice in the mind determined in the way that the wise man would determine it.

Ad 1. It should be said that Augustine is speaking of the virtues ordered to eternal happiness.

Ad 2, 3, 4. The same remark applies to these.

Ad 5. It should be said that acquired virtue does not cause us always to turn from sin, but only for the most part, just as things that come about naturally are only for the most part. But it does not follow from this that anyone is simultaneously vicious and virtuous, because one act of a power does not remove the acquired habit of vice or virtue, and one cannot by acquired virtue avoid every sin. Through acquired virtue, the sin of infidelity is not avoided, nor the other sins opposed to the infused virtues.

Ad 6. It should be said that we do not arrive at heavenly bliss by means of the acquired virtues, but at a certain happiness that a man has been fashioned to achieve in this life by what is naturally proper to him according to the act of perfect virtue of which Aristotle treats in *Ethics* 10.

Ad 7. It should be said that acquired virtue is not the greatest good simply speaking, but the greatest among human goods; infused virtue is the greatest good simply speaking, since by it a man is ordered to the highest good, which is God.

Ad 8. It should be said that a thing considered in the same way cannot form itself, but when there is in a thing one principle that is active and another that is passive, it can form itself partly, namely, such that one of its parts forms and another is formed, just as something moves itself insofar as one of its parts is mover and another moved, as is said in *Physics* 8. So it is in the generation of virtue, as has been shown.

Ad 9. It should be said that science is acquired by intellect not only by discovery but also by teaching, which is from another; so too in the acquisition of virtue, a man is helped by correction and discipline, which are from another. The less one needs these, the more disposed to virtue he is, just as the more one is ingenious of mind, the less need he has of external doctrine.

Ad 10. It should be said that active and passive powers come together in man's action, and something comes forth from the powers insofar as they are active and nothing is received by them; to the passive as passive it falls to acquire something by way of receiving. Hence, in a power which is active alone, such as the agent intellect, no habit is acquired by action.

Ad 11. It should be said that the more efficacious the action of the agent, the quicker it induces the form. Thus, in intellectual matters we see that one powerful demonstration can cause science in us. But opinion, though it is less than science, is not caused in us by one dialectical syllogism, but requires many because of their weakness. Hence, in things to be done, because activities of the soul are not efficacious as are demonstrations, because things to be done are contingent and probable, one act does not suffice to cause virtue but many are required. And though these many are not simultaneous, they can still cause a habit, because the first act causes some disposition and the second act, finding the matter disposed, disposes it even more, and third yet more and thus the ultimate act acting in virtue of all the preceding completes the generation of virtue, like the many drops that hollow the stone.

Ad 12. It should be said that Avicenna intends to define natural virtue which follows on the form which is an essential principle; hence, his definition is not apropos.

Ad 13. It should be said that virtue is generated by acts that are in a way virtuous and in a way vicious. For the acts preceding virtue are indeed virtuous with respect to what is done, insofar as a man does brave and just things, but not with respect to the manner of acting, because before acquiring the habit of virtue a man does not do the works of virtue as the virtuous man does, namely, promptly and without doubt and with pleasure and easily.

Ad 14. It should be said that reason is more noble than the virtue generated in the appetitive part, since such a virtue is only caused by a certain participation in reason. Therefore, the act which precedes virtue can cause virtue insofar as it is from reason, which confers that which is of perfection in it. For its imperfection is in the appetitive power in which the habit is not yet caused by which a man with pleasure and with expedition brings off that which is commanded by reason.

Ad 15. It should be said that virtue is said to be the utmost of a power, not because it is always something of the essence of the power, but because it inclines to that of which the power is ultimately capable.

Ad 16. It should be said that man is good according to his own nature in a manner of speaking, not absolutely. In order for something to be absolutely good it must be totally perfected, just as in order for something to be beautiful absolutely there must be no deformity or defilement in any part. Someone is called simply and totally good because he has a good will, because it is by will that a man uses all the other powers. Therefore, a good will makes a man good simply speaking, and because of this the virtue of the appetitive part, thanks to which the will becomes good, is that which simply speaking makes the one having it good.

Ad 17. It should be said that the acts which are prior to virtue can indeed be called natural because they proceed from natural reason, insofar as natural is distinguished from acquired. But they cannot be called natural insofar as natural is distinguished from what is of reason. Thus, it is said that we do not become accustomed, or the opposite, to what is natural, insofar as nature is distinguished from reason.

Ad 18. It should be said that grace is called the form of infused virtue, not because it gives it its specific being, but insofar as by it its act is informed in a certain way. Hence, there is no need that political virtue be had by the infusion of grace.

Ad 19. It should be said that virtue is made strong in weakness, not because weakness causes virtue, but because it provides an occasion for some virtue, namely, humility. It is also the matter of a virtue, namely, patience, and even of charity, insofar as someone ministers to the weakness of his neighbor. And it is naturally a sign of virtue, because the more virtuous the soul the less effort is required to move the body to the act of virtue.

Ad 20. It should be said that properly speaking a thing is not said to be altered when it acquires its proper perfection. Thus, since virtue is man's proper perfection, a man is not said to be altered when he acquires virtue, save perhaps incidentally, insofar as the alteration of the sensible part of the soul which is the seat of the soul's emotions pertains to virtue.

Ad 21. It should be said that a man can be said to be such and such [*qualis*] or according to a quality which is in the intellective part, and this is not from the natural make-up of the body nor the influence of the heavenly bodies since the intellective part is free of any body. Or a man can be called such and such according to a disposition in the sensitive part, which can indeed be due to the natural make-up of the body, or from the influence of celestial bodies. However, since this part naturally obeys reason, it can be diminished by custom or even totally removed.

Ad 22. From this the response to 22 is evident, for according to the disposition that is in the sensitive part, some are said to have a natural inclination to vice or virtue, etc.

Article 10

Does a man have any infused virtues?

It seems that he does not.

1. In *Physics* 7 it is said that a thing is perfect when it has achieved its proper virtue. But the proper virtue of anything is its natural perfection. Therefore, for man's perfection the virtue connatural to him is sufficient, and this is what can be brought about by natural principles. Therefore, man does not require for his perfection any virtue had by infusion.

2. But it might be said that man must be perfected not only with respect to the connatural end, but also to the supernatural, which is the happiness of eternal life, to which a man is ordered by the infused virtues. On the contrary: Nature is not deficient in what is necessary. What a man needs for the attainment of the ultimate end is necessary for him. Therefore, he can attain it through natural principles and has no need of the infusion of virtue.

3. Moreover, seed acts by the power of that which emits it; otherwise animal seed, since it is imperfect, could not by its action produce something perfect in species. But the seeds of the virtues are put into us by God, for as we read in the gloss, God sowed in every soul the beginning of understanding and wisdom. Therefore, seeds of this sort act with the power of God, and since acquired virtues are caused by these seeds, it seems that acquired virtue can lead to the enjoyment of God, in which the happiness of eternal life consists.

4. Insofar as it is meritorious, virtue orders man to the happiness of eternal life. But the acts of the acquired virtues can merit eternal life insofar as they are informed by grace. Therefore, infused virtues are not necessary in order to attain the happiness of eternal life.

5. Moreover, at the root of meriting is charity. Therefore, if it were necessary to have infused virtues to merit eternal life, it seems that charity alone would suffice, and then it would be unnecessary to have the other infused virtues.

6. Moreover, moral virtues are necessary if the lower powers are to be subject to reason, but they are sufficiently subjected to reason by acquired virtues. Therefore, it is not necessary that there should be any infused moral virtues in order that reason be ordered to some

special end, but it suffices that man's reason be directed to that supernatural end. But this comes about sufficiently through faith. Therefore, it is not necessary to have any other infused virtues.

7. Moreover, that which comes about by divine power does not differ in species from that which comes about by the operation of nature. For the health whereby someone is miraculously cured and that which nature produces are of the same species. Therefore, if there were some infused virtue, which is in us from God, and one acquired by our actions, they would not differ specifically; for example, if there is an acquired and an infused temperance. But two forms of the same species cannot simultaneously be in the same subject. Therefore, it cannot be that someone who has acquired temperance should have infused temperance.

8. Moreover, the species of a virtue is known from its acts. But the acts of infused and acquired temperance are specifically the same; therefore, the virtues are specifically the same. But the acts of infused and of acquired temperance agree in matter, for both concern things pleasant to touch. But they also agree in form, because each consists in the mean. Therefore, the act of infused temperance and the act of acquired temperance are specifically the same.

9. But it might be said that they differ specifically because they are ordered to different ends and in moral matters the species is derived from the end. On the contrary: Things will differ specifically in terms of that from which the species is derived. But species in moral matters is not taken from ultimate end, but from the proximate end, otherwise all virtues would be specifically the same, since they are all ordered to happiness as to their ultimate end. Therefore, it cannot be said that in morals things are of the same species, or of different species, because of their order to ultimate end, and thus infused temperance does not specifically differ from acquired temperance from the fact that it orders man to a higher happiness.

10. Moreover, no moral habit takes its species from the fact that it is moved by some habit, for it happens that one moral habit is moved or commanded by others which are specifically different, as the habit of intemperance is moved by the habit of avarice when a person commits adultery in order to steal and another kills in order to steal. But temperance or courage or any other moral virtue does

not have an act ordered to the happiness of eternal life unless it is commanded by a virtue which has the ultimate end for its object. Therefore, it does not takes its species from that, and thus the infused moral virtue does not specifically differ from acquired virtue because through it one is ordered to the end of eternal life.

11. Moreover, infused virtue is in mind as in a subject, for Augustine says that virtue is the good quality of mind which God brings about in us without us. But moral virtues are not in mind as in subject, for temperance and fortitude are in the irrational parts, as the Philosopher says in *Ethics* 3. Therefore, moral virtues are not infused.

12. Moreover, contraries share the same notion. But vice which is the contrary of virtue is never infused, but is only caused by our acts. Therefore, neither are virtues infused, but they too are caused only by our acts.

13. Moreover, before acquiring it a man is in potency to virtue, but potency and act are in the same genus, for every genus is divided by potency and act, as is evident in the *Physics*. Therefore, since the potentiality for virtue is not in us by infusion, it seems that neither is virtue in us from infusion.

14. Moreover, if the virtues are infused, it is necessary that they be infused at the same time. But when grace is actually infused in a man who was in sin, the moral virtues are not then infused in him, for he can still be bothered by the passions after contrition, which is not true of the virtuous person though perhaps of the continent: The continent man differs from the temperate in this, that the former is still affected though not misled, whereas the temperate is no longer affected, as is said in *Ethics* 7. Therefore, it seems that virtues are not in us by the infusion of grace.

15. Moreover, as the Philosopher says in *Ethics* 2, it is sign that a habit has been acquired that it causes pleasant activity; but after contrition one does not immediately take pleasure in the acts of moral virtue. Therefore, he does not yet have the habit of the virtues and moral virtues are not caused in us by the infusion of grace.

16. Moreover, we hold that a vicious habit is caused in a person by many bad acts. It is manifest that by one act of contrition sins are taken away and grace infused, whereas an acquired habit is not de-

stroyed by one act, nor acquired by one act. Therefore, since the moral virtues are infused at the same time as grace, it follows that the habits of moral virtues must coexist with their opposite habits, which is impossible.

17. Moreover, a virtue is generated and corrupted by the same thing, as is said in *Ethics* 3. Therefore, if virtue is not caused in us by our acts, it would seem to follow that it cannot be corrupted by our acts, and it would then follow that one sinning mortally does not lose virtue, which is absurd.

18. Moreover, mores and customs seem to be the same. Therefore, moral virtue and custom are the same. But virtue is called custom from 'becoming accustomed,' for it is caused by often acting well. Therefore, every moral virtue is caused by acts and none by the infusion of grace.

19. Moreover, if some virtues are infused, it is necessary that their acts are more efficacious than the acts of a man not having virtues. But it is from acts of the same kind that a habit of virtue is caused in us. Therefore, from the acts of infused virtues, if there are any, the same would be true. But it is said in *Ethics* 2 that as the habits, so the acts, and as the acts, so the habits they cause. Therefore, the habits caused by acts of infused virtues are of the same species as the infused virtues, and it would follow that two forms of the same species are simultaneously in the same subject, which is impossible. Therefore it seems to be impossible that there are any infused virtues in us.

ON THE CONTRARY. 1. It is said in Luke 24, 49, "But wait here in the city, until you are clothed with power from on high."

2. Moreover, in Wisdom 8, 7, speaking of divine wisdom, the author says, "For she teacheth temperance and prudence and justice and fortitude . . ." by causing them. Therefore, it seems that there are moral virtues infused in us by God.

3. Moreover, the acts of any virtue ought to be meritorious in order that we might be led by them to happiness. But there can be no merit except from grace. Therefore, it seems that the virtues are caused in us by the infusion of grace.

RESPONSE. It should be said that, over and above the virtues that are acquired by our acts, it is necessary to recognize other virtues infused in man by God, as has been said. The reason for this can be sought in this, that virtue, as the Philosopher says, is what makes the one having it good and makes his work good. Therefore, insofar as the good is diversified in man, it is necessary that virtue too be diversified, since it is clear that the good of man as man is different from the good of man as citizen. It is manifest that some operations can be fitting to man insofar as he is man which are not fitting to him insofar as he is a citizen. For this reason the Philosopher says in *Politics* 3 that the virtue that makes a man good is other than that which makes the good citizen. It should be noticed, however, that there is a twofold good of man, one which is proportioned to his nature, another which exceeds the capacity of his nature. The reason for this is that what is passive must acquire perfections from the agent differently according to the diversity of the agent's power. Hence, we see that the perfections and forms which are caused by the action of the natural agent do not exceed the natural capacity of the recipient, for the natural active power is proportioned to the potencies of the natural recipient.

But the perfections and forms which come from a supernatural agent of infinite power, that is, from God, exceed the capacity of the receiving nature. Hence, the rational soul, which is immediately caused by God, exceeds the capacity of its matter, such that bodily matter cannot completely comprehend and include it, but there remains some power and operation of it in which bodily matter does not share, which is not the case with any of the other forms which are caused by natural agents. But just as man acquires his first perfection, that is, his soul, by the action of God, so too he has his ultimate perfection, which is his perfect happiness, immediately from God, and rests in it. Indeed this is obvious from the fact that man's natural desire cannot rest in anything else save in God alone.

For it is innate in man that he be moved by a desire to go on from what has been caused and inquire into causes, nor does this desire rest until it arrives at the first cause, which is God. Therefore, it is necessary that, just as man's first perfection, which is the rational soul, exceeds the capacity of bodily matter, so the ultimate perfection to which a man can come, which is the happiness of eternal life, should exceed the entire capacity of human nature. And because a thing is ordered to its end by some activity, and those things which are for the sake of the end must be proportioned to the end, it is necessary that there should be some perfections of man whereby he is ordered to the supernatural end which exceeds the capacity of man's natural principles.

But this can only be if over and above the natural principles there are supernatural principles of action infused in man by God. The natural principles of operation are the essence of the soul and its powers, namely, intellect and will, which are the principles of man's activity as such. And this is so because intellect has knowledge of the principles by which it might be directed to other things and will has a natural inclination to the good proportioned to its nature, as was argued in the preceding question. Therefore, in order that a man might perform actions ordered to the end of eternal life, there is divinely infused in him first grace, by which the soul has a kind of spiritual existence, and then faith, hope, and charity, so that by faith the intellect is illumined by certain things known supernaturally, which are in this order as the principles naturally known in the order of connatural activities, and by hope and charity the will acquires a certain inclination to that supernatural good to which the human will is insufficiently ordered by its natural inclination.

Thus, over and above the natural principles by which the habits of virtue are acquired for man's natural perfection in a manner connatural to him, as has been said above, man acquired by divine influence, beyond the supernatural principles mentioned, certain infused virtues by which he is perfected in operations ordered to the end of eternal life.

Ad 1. It should be said that a man is perfected in two ways when he first comes into being. First, with respect to the nutritive and sensitive powers, by a perfection that does not indeed exceed the capacity of corporeal matter. Second, with respect to the intellective part which does exceed the natural and bodily. It is by the latter that a man is perfect simply speaking, but by the former only in a certain respect. So too a man can be perfected in two ways with respect to the perfection of the end of man, first, according to the capacity of his nature and, second, by a supernatural perfection. It is by the latter that a man is called perfect simply speaking, but by the former only in a certain respect. So it is that man has a twofold virtue, one that answers to the first perfection, which is not virtue in the fullest sense, and another that answers to ultimate perfection, and this is the true and perfect virtue of man.

Ad 2. It should be said that nature provides man with what is necessary according to his power; hence, with respect to the things which do not exceed the capacity of nature, a man has from nature not only receptive principles but also active principles. But with respect to the things which exceed the capacity of his nature, a man has from nature only an aptitude to receive.

Ad 3. It should be said that man's seed acts according to the whole power of man, but the seeds of the virtues naturally placed in human nature do not act according to the whole power of God; hence, it does not follow that they can cause whatever God can cause.

Ad 4. It should be said that since there is no merit without charity, the act of acquired virtue cannot be meritorious without charity. But other virtues are infused along with charity; hence, the act of acquired virtue can only be meritorious by the mediation of infused virtue. For the virtue ordered to an inferior end does not produce an act ordered to the superior end without the mediation of the superior virtue. Just as courage, which is a virtue of man as man, does not order its act to the political good except by the mediation of the courage, which is the virtue of man insofar as he is a citizen.

Ad 5. It should be said that when an action proceeds from several agents ordered to one another, its perfection and goodness can be impeded by one of those agents, even if the other is perfect; however perfect the artisan he does not cause perfect operation if there is a defective instrument. In human activities which become good thanks to virtue, this must be taken into account: The action of the higher power does not depend on the inferior power, but the action of the inferior depends on the superior. Therefore, in order for the acts of the inferior powers – the irascible and concupiscible – to be perfect, not only must intellect be ordered to the ultimate end by faith, and the will by charity, but the inferior powers too, namely, the irascible and concupiscible, have their own activities in order that their acts might be good and orderable to the ultimate end.

Ad 6. The response to the sixth is clear from this.

Ad 7. It should be said that God can produce a form of the same kind that nature produces by himself without the operation of nature. For this reason, the health which is brought about miraculously by God is of the same species as the health that nature causes. Hence, it does not follow that every form that God can make can also be made by nature, nor is it necessary that infused virtue, which is immediately from God, should be of the same species as acquired virtue.

Ad 8. It should be said that infused and acquired temperance agree in matter, for both are concerned with what is pleasant to touch, but they do not agree in the form of their effects or acts, for although each seeks the mean, infused temperance attains it in one way and acquired temperance in another. For infused temperance seeks the mean according to the reasons of divine law, which are taken from their order to the ultimate end, but acquired temperance takes its mean according to inferior reasons, as ordered to the good of the present life.

Ad 9. It should be said that the ultimate end does not specify in moral matters except insofar as there is a due proportion to the ultimate end on the part of the proximate end. For the things which are for the sake of the end must be proportioned to the end, something the goodness of counsel also requires in order that one might decide on the fitting means to the end, as is clear from the Philosopher in *Metaphysics* 6.

Ad 10. It should be said that the act of any habit, as commanded by that habit, takes its moral species, formally speaking, from the act itself. Hence, when one fornicates in order to steal, although his act is materially one of intemperance, it is formally one of avarice, for it is not specific to intemperance that its act be commanded by avarice. But insofar as an act of temperance or courage is commanded by charity ordering it to the ultimate end, the acts formally are specified and formally speaking become acts of charity, but it does not follow that it is from this that temperance and courage are specified. Therefore, infused temperance and courage do not differ specifically from the acquired in this, that their acts are commanded by charity, but rather because their acts are constituted in a mean orderable to the ultimate end which is the object of charity.

Ad 11. It should be said that infused temperance is in the irascible, but the irascible and concupiscible take on the name of reason or rational insofar as they share in some way in reason, that is, by obeying it. Therefore, they have the name of mind in the same way, insofar as they obey mind, so what Augustine says is true: Infused virtue is a good quality of mind.

Ad 12. It should be said that man's vice comes about when he is reduced to inferior things, but his virtue when he is elevated to the higher. That is why only virtue, and not vice, can be from infusion.

Ad 13. It should be said that when something passive is fashioned to acquire different perfections from different ordered agents, there is a difference and order of passive powers in the recipient responding to the difference and order of the active powers of the agents, because the passive power responds to the active. Thus, it is that water or earth have a potency according to which they are moved by fire, and another insofar as they are fashioned to be moved by the heavenly body, and yet another according to which they can be moved by God. For water or earth can become something in virtue of a supernatural agent that they cannot become by the power of a natural agent. For this reason we say that in every creature there is an obediential potency, insofar as every creature obeys God in receiving whatever God wills. There is in the soul a potency fashioned to be actuated by a connatural agent, and in this way it is in potency to acquired virtues. In another way there is a potency in the soul which is fashioned to be actuated only by the divine power, and in this way the infused virtues are potentially in the soul.

Ad 14. It should be said that passions inclining to evil are not completely taken away by either acquired or infused virtue, except maybe miraculously. There always remains the struggle between the flesh and the spirit, even with moral virtue. The Apostle speaks of this in Galatians 5, 17: "For the flesh lusts against the spirit, and the spirit against the flesh." But these passions are modified by both acquired and infused virtue, such that a man is not moved by them in an unbridled way, but acquired virtue in some degree prevails and so too infused virtue. Acquired virtue prevails in this, that the struggle is felt less, and this is due to its cause, since it is by frequent acts that a man is accustomed to virtue, and a man becomes unaccustomed to obey such passions when he has learned to resist them and that is why he feels their troubling less.

But infused virtue prevails in this, that while such passions are felt they in no way dominate, for infused virtue brings it about that the concupiscence of sin is in no way obeyed, and while it remains, it does this infallibly. But acquired virtue fails in this, though rarely, just as other natural inclinations fail infrequently. Hence, the Apostle says in Romans 7, 5, "For when we were in the flesh, the sinful passions which were aroused by the Law, were at work in our members so that they brought forth fruit unto death. But now we have been set free from the Law, having died to that by which we were held down, so that we may serve in a new spirit and not according to the outworn letter."

Ad 15. It should be said that because from the outset infused virtue does not always take away the feeling of the passions like acquired virtue, they are not from the outset performed with pleasure, but this is not out of keeping with what is meant by virtue, because sometimes it suffices for virtue that we act without sadness, and it is not required that we act with pleasure or fail to feel annoyance. The Philosopher says in *Ethics* 3 that it is enough if the brave man acts without sadness.

Ad 16. It should be said that an acquired habit is not corrupted by one simple act; still the act of contrition corrupts the habit of vice through the power of grace. Thus, in one who has the habit of intemperance and is contrite there does not remain with the virtue of infused temperance the habit of intemperance in the sense of a habit, but it is on the way to corruption, as a certain disposition. But a disposition is not the contrary of a perfect habit.

Ad 17. It should be said that, although infused virtue is not caused by acts, still acts can dispose to it, hence it is not unfitting that it be corrupted by acts, because form is taken away by the indisposition of matter, as the soul is separated from body because of the indisposition of matter.

Ad 18. It should be said that moral virtue is not named from *mos* insofar as it signifies the accustoming of the appetitive power, for in this way the infused virtue could be called moral, although they are not caused by accustoming.

Ad 19. It should be said that the acts of infused virtue do not cause a habit, but due to them pre-existing habits are increased. No more by the acts of acquired virtue is any habit generated, otherwise habits would be multiplied ad infinitum.

Article 11
Whether infused virtue can increase

It seems that it cannot.

1. Only what is quantified increases. But virtue is a quality, is not a quantity. Therefore it does not increase.

2. Moreover, virtue is an accidental form, but form is most simple and consists of an invariable essence. Therefore, virtue does not vary in its essence and cannot increase in its essence.

3. Morever, that which increases, changes. Therefore, what increases in its essence changes in its essence, and what changes in its essence is corrupted or generated. But generation and corruption are changes in substance. Therefore, charity is not increased in essence except when it is generated or corrupted.

4. Moreover, essentials do not increase or diminish. But it is manifest that the essence of virtue is essential. Therefore, virtue does not increase in its essence.

5. Moreover, contraries are such as to come to be in the same subject. But increase and decrease are contraries which come about in the same thing. But infused virtue does not diminish since it is neither diminished by the act of virtue, which rather strengthens it, nor by the fact of venial sin, since then many venial sins would totally take away charity and the other infused virtues, which is impossible, for then many venial sins would equal one mortal sin, nor are they diminished by mortal sin, since mortal sin takes away charity and the other infused virtues. Therefore, an infused virtue does not increase.

6. Moreover, a thing is increased by something similar to itself, as is said in *On the soul* 2. Therefore, if the infused virtue increased, it would have to increase by the addition of virtue. But this cannot be, because virtue is simple, and a simple added to the simple does not make it greater, as a point added to a point does not make a greater line. Therefore, infused virtue cannot be increased.

7. Moreover, in *On generation and corruption* 1 it is said that growth is addition to a pre-existent magnitude. Therefore, if virtue increased, something would have to be added to it, and thus it would be a greater composite and more distant from the divine similitude

and consequently less good, which is ridiculous. Therefore, virtue does not increase.

8. Moreover, whatever is increased is moved, and whatever is moved is a body. But virtue is not a body. Therefore, it is not increased.

9. Moreover, that whose cause is invariable is itself invariable. But the cause of infused virtue, which is God, is invariable. Therefore, infused virtue is invariable and is not susceptible of more or less and does not increase.

10. Moreover, virtue like science is in the genus of habit. Therefore, if virtue increased, it would be necessary that it increase in the way that science does. But science is increased by the multiplication of objects, that is, it extends to more things. That this is not how virtue increases is clear from charity, since the least charity extends to loving all things charitably. Therefore, virtue in no way increases.

11. Moreover, if virtue increased, its increase would have to belong to some type of change. But it could only belong to alteration, which is change according to quality, but alteration, according to the Philosopher in *Physics* 7, is only in the sensitive part of the soul which is not where charity or any of the other infused virtues resides. Therefore, not every infused virtue increases.

12. Moreover, if infused virtue increased, it would have to be increased by God, who causes it, but if God increased it, this would have to be by a new infusion, but this can only be a new infused virtue. Therefore, an infused virtue can only be increased by the addition of a new virtue, but that it cannot be increased in this way was shown above. Therefore, the infused virtue cannot be increased in any way.

13. Moreover, it is by its acts that a habit is maximally increased. But this, it seems, cannot be, since the act comes forth from the habit, and nothing is increased by what goes forth from it but rather by what it receives. Therefore, virtue can in no way increase.

14. Moreover, the acts of the same virtue are the same. Therefore, if a virtue were increased by its acts, it would have to be increased by each of them, which seems falsified by experience. We do not experience an increase of virtue from each of its acts.

15. Moreover, things whose notion consists in the superlative cannot be increased: There is no better than the best, nor whiter than the whitest. But the notion of virtue consists in the superlative, for it is the utmost of a power. Therefore, virtue cannot be increased.

16. Moreover, that whose definition consists in some indivisible lacks intension or remission, for example, substantial form, number, and figure. But the notion of virtue consists in something indivisible, for it lies in the mean. Therefore, virtue is neither intensified not lessened.

17. Moreover, nothing that is infinite can be increased, since there is nothing greater than it. But infused virtue is infinite because through it a man merits an infinite good, namely, God. Therefore, infused virtue cannot be increased.

18. Moreover, nothing extends beyond its own perfection because its perfection is the limit of the thing, but virtue is the perfection of the one having it, for it is said in *Physics* 7 that virtue is the disposition of the perfect to the best. Therefore, virtue does not increase.

ON THE CONTRARY. 1. In 1 Peter 2, 2, "Crave, as newborn babes, pure spiritual milk, that by it you may grow to salvation." But no one grows in health save through an increase of virtue by which man is ordered to salvation. Therefore, virtue increases.

2. Moreover, Augustine says that charity increases in order that as increased it might merit perfection.

RESPONSE. It should be said that many errors are made about forms when they are thought of as substances. This seems to happen because forms are abstractly signified in the mode of substance, e.g., whiteness, or virtue and the like. So some following the mode of expression judge them as if they were substances and from this arises the error both of those which held the latency of forms and of those who held forms to have been from creation, for they thought that becoming belonged to forms as it does to substances, and thus unable to find anything from which forms could be generated, they held that they were created or pre-existed in matter, not taking into account that just as existence is not of the form but of the subject through the form, neither does the becoming that terminates in existence pertain to form but to the subject. For just as form is called being, not because it exists, properly speaking, but because something exists by it, so form is said to come to be, not because it becomes, but because by it something comes to be, namely, when the subject is reduced from potency to act.

So it is with respect to increase of qualities, of which some have spoken as if qualities and forms were substances; substance is said to increase insofar as it is the subject of a motion going from a lesser to a greater quantity, a motion called increase. And because the increase of substance comes about by the addition of substance to substance, some thought that in this way charity or any infused virtue is increased by the addition of charity to charity, or of virtue to virtue, or of whiteness to whiteness, which can in no way be defended. For the addition of one to another can only be understood if duality is presupposed. But the duality of forms of the same species can only be understood as the otherness of subject. Therefore, if quality were added to quality, one of these must exist: Either such that subject is added to subject, for example one white thing is added to another white thing, or that something in the subject becomes white which previously was not, as some held of bodily qualities, which the Philosopher disproved in *Physics* 4. For when something becomes more curved, it is not that something that previously was not curved becomes curved, but that a whole becomes more curved. With regard to spiritual qualities, whose subject is the soul, or a part of the soul, it is impossible to imagine this. Hence, others said that charity and the other infused virtues are not increased essentially, but that they are said to be increased either insofar as they are more strongly rooted in the subject or insofar as they are more fervently or intensely performed. This would make sense if charity were a substance having existence of itself apart from substance. Hence, the Master of the *Sentences*, thinking charity to be a substance, namely, the Holy Spirit himself, not unreasonably seems to posit this manner of increase; but others, thinking charity to be a quality, spoke quite unreasonably. For a quality to be increased is nothing other than for a subject to participate more in a quality, for the quality has no existence save in a subject.

Because a subject participates more in a quality, it acts more vehemently and since anything acts insofar as it is in act, that which is more reduced to act acts more perfectly. Therefore, to hold that a quality does not increase in essence, but increases by rootedness in its subject or according to intension of act is to hold that contradictories simultaneously exist. So it remains to be asked how some qualities and forms are said to increase, and which of them can. Note, therefore, that since names are signs of concepts, as is said in *On interpretation*, just as from the more known we know the less known, so too we name the less known from the more known. Hence, it is that because local motion is the most obvious of the motions, from the contrariety of place the word distance is extended to all contraries between which there can be some motion, as the Philosopher says in *Metaphysics* 10.

Similarly, because the quantitative change of a substance is more sensible than its alteration, names appropriate to quantitative change are extended to alteration. So it is that, just as a body that moves to its perfect quantity is said to increase in quantity, and the perfect quantity is said to be large with respect to the imperfect, so too what is changed from imperfect to perfect quality is said to increase in quality, and its perfect quality is called greater with respect to the imperfect. And, because a thing's perfection is its goodness, Augustine says that greater is better in things that are not much. To be changed from imperfect to perfect form is nothing other than for the subject to become more actual, for its act is form, and for a subject to receive more form is for it to be more actual with respect to that form. And just as it is brought by an agent from pure potency to the act of the form, so it is by the action of the agent also that it is brought from imperfect to perfect act.

But this is not true of all forms, and for two reasons.

First, because of the very meaning of form. What completes the definition of a form is something indivisible, like a number, for an added unit constitutes a species, which is why there is not more or less of two and three. Consequently, more and less are not found in quantities denominated from numbers, for example, two inches or three inches, nor in figures, for example, triangle and square, nor in proportions, for example, double and triple.

Second, because of the comparison of form to its subject, in which it inheres in an indivisible manner. For this reason a substantial form is not subject to intensification or diminution, because it gives substantial existence, which is in a single manner: where there is a different substantial existence, there is a different thing. That is why Aristotle in *Metaphysics 8* likens definitions to numbers. Likewise, nothing that is predicated substantially of another, even if it is in a category of accident, is predicated according to more or less. For example, whiteness is not said to be more or less color. Because of this, even qualities abstractly signified, which is for them to be signified in the manner of substance, are not subject to intensification or its opposite: It is not whiteness that is said to be more or less, but a white thing.

However, neither of these is applicable to charity or the other infused virtues, preventing them to be more or less intense. Their definition does not consist in an indivisible, nor do they give substantial existence to their subjects, as substantial forms do. Therefore they can be more or less intense insofar as their subject is made more or less actual by them thanks to the agent causing them. Hence, just as acquired virtues are increased by the acts which cause them, so infused virtues are increased by the action of God by whom they are caused.

Our actions dispose to the increase of charity and the infused virtues, in the way that charity is obtained from the outset. A man who does what it is in his power prepares himself so that he might receive charity from God. Furthermore, our acts can merit an increase of charity, insofar as they presuppose charity which is the principle of meriting. But no one can merit charity at the outset, because without charity there can be no merit. It is in this way, then, that we say that charity can be increased in intensity.

Ad 1. It should be said that just as we speak of increase in charity and other qualities by way of similarity, so too do we attribute quantity to them, as is clear from what has been said.

Ad 2. It should be said that form is invariable because it is not subject to variation, but it can be called variable insofar as its subject is varied and participates in it more and less.

Ad 3. It should be said that the motion of a thing can be understood to be according to essence in two ways. In one way, with respect to that which is proper, namely, essential existence or non-existence, and this motion according to essence is nothing other than motion with respect to existence and non-existence, that is, generation and corruption. In another way motion according to essence can be understood to be according to something adhering to the essence, as we say that a body is moved essentially when it is moved according to place, because its subject is transferred from place to place. Just so a quality is said to be changed essentially in its own way insofar as it varies when the subject has more or less of it, as has been explained in the Response.

Ad 4. It should be said that what is predicated essentially of charity is not predicated according to more and less, for it is not said to be more or less a virtue, But greater charity is said to be more a virtue on account of the mode of signifying, because it is signified as a substance; still, because it is not predicated essentially of its subject, what is subject to it receives more and less, as a subject having more or less charity, and what has more charity is more virtuous.

Ad 5. It should be said that charity is not diminished because it does not have a cause of decrease, as Ambrose proves. But it has a cause of increase, namely, God.

Ad 6. It should be said that the increase that comes about through addition is increase of the quantified substance. But charity does not increase in this way, as was said in the body of the article.

Ad 7. From which the answer to 7 is clear.

Ad 8. It should be said that charity is said to be increased or changed, not because it is the subject of motion, but because its subject is moved or increased in its regard.

Ad 9. It should be said that although God is invariable yet he varies things without varying himself. For it is not necessary that every mover be moved, as is proved in the *Physics*. And this belongs chiefly to God, because he does not act from any necessity of nature, but by his will.

Ad 10. It should be said that the notion of magnitude mentioned is common to all qualities and forms, namely, their perfection in the subject. Other qualities, apart from this magnitude or the quality belonging to them as such, have another magnitude or quantity which belongs to them accidentally. And this in two ways. In one way, by reason of the subject, as whiteness is quantified incidentally because its subject is quantified; hence, when the subject is increased, the whiteness increases incidentally. But on this basis when something is called whiter, it is not said to be more of a white thing but of a greater whiteness. For what pertains to increase in this sense is not said otherwise of white and of the subject, because its whiteness is said accidentally to increase. But this kind of quantity and increase does not belong to qualities of the soul such as sciences and virtues.

In another way quantity and increase are attributed incidentally to a quality because of the object on which it acts, and this is called the quantity of virtue or power, which refers to the quantity of the object or container, as that is said to be of great power which can bear a great weight, or can do something big in whatever sense, whether by dimensive magnitude or the magnitude of perfection, or according to discrete quantity, as that is said to be of great power which can do many things. In this way quantity can be incidentally attributed to the qualities of the soul, that is, to sciences and virtues. But there is this difference between science and virtue, that it is not of the notion of science that it actually extend to all objects, for it is not necessary that the knower know all knowable things. But it is of the essence of virtue that it always acts virtuously. Hence, science can be increased either according to the number of objects or according to its intensity in the subject, but virtue in one way only. But it should be considered that it is for the same reason that some quality can be referred to something great, and that it is itself great, as is clear from the foregoing; hence, the magnitude of perfection can also be called the magnitude of virtue.

Ad 11. It should be said that the motion of increase of charity is reduced to alteration, not insofar as alteration is between contraries, as it always is in sensible things, and in the sensible part of the soul, but insofar as alteration and passion refer to reception and perfection, as sensing and understanding are a kind of receiving and being altered. Thus, the Philosopher distinguishes alteration and passion in *On the soul* 2.

Ad 12. It should be said that God increases charity not by infusing new charity but by perfecting that which already exists.

Ad 13. It should be said that just as the act coming forth from an agent can cause acquired virtue because of the impression of active powers on the passive, as was said above, so too it can increase it.

Ad 14. It should be said that charity and the other infused virtues are not increased actively by acts, but only dispositively and meritoriously, as has been said. However, it is not necessary that any perfect act correspond to the quantity of virtue, for it is not necessary that one having charity should always act according to the full force of charity; the use of habits is subject to will.

Ad 15. It should be said that the notion of virtue does not consist in the superlative with respect to itself, but with respect to its object, because by virtue a man is ordered to the utmost of a power, which is to act well; hence, the Philosopher says in *Physics* 7 that virtue is the disposition of the perfected to the best. However, one can be more or less disposed to this optimum, and in this respect, virtue receives more or less. Or it might be said that it is not called the utmost simply, but the utmost of a kind, as fire is in kind the most subtle body and man the most worthy of creatures, yet one man is more worthy than another.

Ad 16. It should be said that the notion of virtue does not consist in the indivisible in itself, but by reason of its subject, insofar as it seeks the mean, for the seeking of which it can comport itself in different ways, well or badly. However, the mean itself is not in every way indivisible, but has a certain latitude, since it suffices for virtue that it approach the mean, as is said in *Ethics* 2, and for this reason one act is said to be more virtuous than another.

Ad 17. It should be said that the virtue of charity with respect to its end, God, is infinite, but charity finitely disposes to that end and hence is susceptible of more or less.

Ad 18. Not every perfect thing is most perfect, but only that which is in ultimate actuality; thus there is no impediment to someone already perfected by virtue to become more perfect.

Article 12
On the distinction of the virtues

It seems that the virtues are not rightly distinguished.

1. Moral matters are specified by the end. Therefore, if virtues are specifically different, this must be on the part of the end. But not of the proximate end, because thus there would be an infinity of species of virtues. Therefore, of the ultimate end. But the ultimate end of the virtues is one alone, namely, God, or happiness. Therefore, there is only one virtue.

2. Moreover, one activity has one end. But an activity is one from one form; therefore, a man is ordered to one end by one form. But man's end is one, namely, happiness. So virtue too is one, which is the form by which a man is ordered to happiness.

3. Moreover, forms and accidents are numbered according to matter or subject. But the subject of virtue is the soul or a power of the soul. It seems, therefore, that virtue is one alone, because the soul is one, or, at least, that virtues do not exceed in number the powers of the soul.

4. Moreover, habits are distinguished by objects, as powers are. Therefore, since the virtues are habits, it seems that there should be the same basis for distinguishing virtues and powers of the soul, and thus the virtues would not exceed the powers of the soul in number.

5. Moreover, it might be said that habits are distinguished by acts and not by powers, but on the contrary: What derive from principles are distinguished by the principles and not the reverse, because a thing has existence and unity from the same cause, but habits are the principles of acts. Therefore, acts are distinguished according to habits rather than conversely.

6. Moreover, virtue is necessary if a man is to be inclined naturally to that with which the virtue is concerned. For, as Cicero says, virtue is a habit in the manner of nature and in harmony with reason. In order for this power to be inclined naturally, therefore, a man does not need virtue, for man's will is naturally inclined to the ultimate end. Therefore, with respect to the ultimate end, man does not need any habit of virtue, for which reason philosophers do not posit any virtues whose object would be happiness. Therefore, we should

not posit such theological virtues either, whose object is God, the ultimate end.

7. Moreover, virtue is the disposition of that which is already somewhat perfected for the best, but faith and hope imply imperfection, because faith is concerned with what is not seen and hope with what is not had, because of which, when it comes to be perfected, "that which is imperfect will be done away with," is said in 1 Corinthians 13, 10. Therefore, faith and hope ought not be placed among the virtues.

8. Moreover, no one can be ordered to God except through intellect and will. But faith sufficiently orders a man's intellect to God and charity his will. Therefore, we ought not posit the theological virtue of hope beyond faith and charity.

9. Moreover, that which is general to every virtue ought not to be posited as a special virtue. But charity seems to be common to all the virtues, because as Augustine says in *On the customs of the church*, virtue is nothing but the order of love. Charity itself is also said to be the form of all virtues, therefore, it ought not be numbered as a special theological virtue.

10. Moreover, in God should be considered not only truth, which faith looks to, or sublimity which, hope looks to, or goodness, which charity looks to – there are many others things attributed to God, such as wisdom, power, and the like. Therefore, it seems that either there is only one theological virtue because all these are one in God, or that there should be as many theological virtues as there are things attributed to God.

11. Moreover, a theological virtue is one whose act is ordered immediately to God, but many other things are like that, such as wisdom which contemplates God, fear which reveres him, religion which honors him. Therefore, there are not just three theological virtues.

12. Moreover, the end is the reason for the things that are for the sake of the end. Therefore, once the theological virtues, whereby man is rightly ordered to God, are had, it seems superfluous to posit other virtues.

13. Moreover, virtue is ordered to the good, for virtue is what makes the one having it good and makes his work good. But since

good is in the will and appetitive part, it seems that there cannot be any intellectual virtues.

14. Moreover, prudence is an intellectual virtue. But it is numbered among the moral virtues, so it seems that moral virtues are not distinguished from the intellectual.

15. Moreover, moral science deals only with moral matters, but moral science treats of the intellectual virtues; therefore, the intellectual virtues are moral.

16. Moreover, what is put into the definition of a thing is not distinguished from it, but prudence is put into the definition of moral virtue, for moral virtue is an elective habit consisting in a mean determined by right reason, as is said in *Ethics* 2. But right reason with respect to things to be done is prudence, as is said in *Ethics* 6. Therefore, the moral virtues are not distinguished from prudence.

17. Both art and prudence pertain to practical knowledge. But art does not require habits in the appetitive part ordered to effecting artificial things. Therefore, by parity of reasoning, there should be no need for virtuous habits in the appetitive part in order that prudence might be effective. Thus, it seems that not are no moral virtues distinct from prudence.

18. Moreover, should it be said that no virtue in appetite answers to art because appetite is of singulars, on the contrary, Aristotle says in *Ethics* 2 that wrath deals with singulars, but hate is also of universals, for we hate the whole genus of thieves. But hate pertains to appetite. Therefore, appetite deals with universals.

19. Moreover, every power naturally tends to its object, but the object of appetite is the known good. Therefore, appetite naturally tends to the good insofar as it is known, but prudence sufficiently perfects us for knowing the good. Therefore, we have no need of any other moral virtue than prudence in appetite, since the natural inclination suffices for this.

20. Moreover, knowledge and action suffice for virtue, but both of these are had in prudence. Therefore, there is no need to posit other moral virtues besides prudence.

21. Moreover, the habits of the cognitive part, like those of the appetitive, are distinguished by their objects. But there is one cognitive habit of all the moral virtues, either one moral science which

concerns all moral matters, or prudence. Therefore, there is only one moral virtue in the appetite.

22. Moreover, things which agree in form and differ only in matter are specifically the same. But all moral virtues agree in that which is formal in them, because in all of them there is a mean accepted from right reason; and they differ only in their matters. Therefore, they do not differ in species but only in number.

23. Moreover, specifically different things are not named from one another. But the moral virtues are denominated from one another. Augustine says that justice must be brave and temperate and temperance just and brave, and so with the rest. Therefore, virtues are not distinct from one another.

24. Moreover, the theological and cardinal virtues rank higher than moral virtues. But the intellectual, not the theological, virtues are said to be cardinal. No more then should the moral virtues be called cardinal, as if they ranked higher.

25. Moreover, the soul has three parts, namely, the rational, the irascible, and the concupiscible. Therefore, if there are principal virtues, it seems that they should be only three in number.

26. Moreover, other virtues seem to rank higher, such as magnanimity which does great things in all the virtues, as is said in *Ethics* 6, and humility, which is the guardian of virtue. Even meekness seems superior to courage, since it governs wrath from which the irascible is denominated; liberality and magnificence, which give of themselves, seem higher than justice, which renders another his due. Therefore, these rather than the others should be the cardinal virtues.

27. Moreover, a part is not distinguished from its whole. But Cicero says that the other virtues are parts of these, namely, of prudence, justice, courage, and temperance. Therefore, at the least the other virtues ought not be distinguished from these, and thus the virtues do not seem to be correctly distinguished.

ON THE CONTRARY. In 1 Corinthians 13, 13, we read, "there remain now these three, faith, hope and charity," and Wisdom 8, 7. "For she teacheth temperance and prudence and justice and fortitude."

RESPONSE. It should be said that a thing is specified by that which is formal in it, and what is formal in a thing is that which completes its definition, for the ultimate difference constitutes the species, which is why the defined differs specifically from others because of it. If this could be formally multiplied according to different notions, the defined would be divided into different species. But what completes and is ultimately formal in the definition of virtue is the good. For taken generally virtue is that which makes the one having it good and makes his action good, as is clear from the *Ethics*. Hence, man's virtue, which is what we are speaking of, will be specifically different insofar as the good is differentiated by reason. But since man is man insofar as he is rational, his good must be in some way rational. But the rational or intellective part comprises both the cognitive and appetitive. However, it is not just the appetite which is in the rational part which follows on the grasp of intellect, that is, will, that pertains to the rational part, but also the appetite in man's sensitive part which is divided into the irascible and concupiscible. For in man this appetite too follows the lead of reason insofar as it obeys the command of reason. That is why it is said to participate in reason. Therefore, man's good is the good of both the cognitive and the appetitive parts.

But good is not attributed to each part in the same sense, for good is formally attributed to the appetitive part, since good is the object of the appetitive part. Good is not attributed formally to the intellective part, but only materially, for to know the true is a good of the cognitive part, although it does not relate to the cognitive part under the formality of the good as it does to the appetitive, for knowledge of truth is desirable. Therefore, the virtue which perfects the cognitive part in knowledge of the true must have a different sense than that which perfects the appetitive in attaining the good, for which reason the Philosopher in the *Ethics* distinguishes the intellectual from the moral virtues. Those are called intellectual which perfect the intellectual part in knowing the true, and those that perfect the appetitive part in seeking the good are called moral. And because the good belongs to the appetitive part more properly than to the intellective, the term virtue more fittingly and properly belongs to the virtues of the appetitive than to the virtues of the intellective, although intellectual virtues are more noble perfections than are the moral virtues, as is said in *Ethics* 6.

But knowledge of the true does not always have the same sense. To know necessary truth is one thing, to know the contingent another, and necessary truth is further subdivided into the self-evident (as when the intellect knows first principles) and that which is known by inference (as intellect knows conclusions by science and the highest things by wisdom: means something different when a man is led on to know other things).

There is also another notion of knowing in them, from the fact that by this a man is directed in knowing other things. And similarly, with respect to contingent things to be done, there is not a single sense of knowing [1] the things that remain in us and are called do-able, as being our operations, concerning which we often err on account of passion and with which prudence is concerned, and [2] things outside us but makeable by us where art is directive and in which the passions of the soul do not vitiate estimation. Therefore, in *Ethics* 6 the Philosopher posits intellectual virtues, namely, wisdom, science, and understanding, prudence and art.

No more does the good of the appetitive part always have the same sense in all human affairs. This good is sought in three kinds of matter, namely, in the passions of the irascible and in the passions of the concupiscible and in our acts which are concerned with external things or things which come into our use, as in buying and selling, placing, guiding, and other like things. Man's good in the case of the passions is that he be so related to them that he does not turn from the judgment of reason because of their influence; hence, if there are passions which are such as to impede the good of reason by mode of inciting to action or pursuit, the good of virtue consists chiefly in a restraint and holding back, as is evident in temperance, which refrains and holds back desires. If, however, a passion is such that it chiefly impedes the good of reason in withdrawal, as in fear, the good of virtue with respect to such a passion consists in sustaining, which is what courage does. With respect to external things, the good of reason consists in this, that they receive a fitting proportion, insofar as they pertain to the sharing of human life, and the word *jus-*

tice is imposed from this, since it directs and discovers equality in such things.

But it should be considered that both the good of the intellectual and of the appetitive part are twofold, namely, the good which is the ultimate end and the good that is for the sake of the end, and these do not have the same sense. Therefore, beyond the virtues mentioned, thanks to which a man pursues the good which is for the sake of the end, there must be other virtues thanks to which he is well related to the ultimate end which is God. That is why they are called theological: They have God not only for their end, but for their object.

In order that we be moved correctly to the end, the end must be known and desired. But the desire of the end requires two things, namely, trust concerning the end to be obtained, because no wise man moves toward that which he cannot attain, and love of the end, because only the loved is desired. There are accordingly three theological virtues, namely, faith, by which we know God, hope, whereby we hope to attain him, and charity, by which we love him. It is clear then that there are three kinds of virtue: theological, intellectual, and moral and that there are several species of each kind.

Ad 1. It should be said that moral matters are specified by proximate ends, which, however, are not infinite if we consider in them only their formal difference. For the proximate end of any virtue is the good that is done by means of it, which goods provide their different definitions, as was shown in the body of the article.

Ad 2. It should be said that the argument works in things which act from the necessity of their nature, since they attain the end by one action and one form. But man has reason because he must reach his end by many different ways, and that is why many virtues are necessary for him.

Ad 3. It should be said that accidents are not multiplied numerically in the same thing, but only specifically; hence, the unity or multitude of virtues ought not be looked for according to their subject, which is the soul, or its potencies, unless a different notion of good follows on the diversity of powers, since virtues are distinguished according to that, as has been said.

Ad 4. It should be said that a thing is not the object of a power and of a habit for the same reason, for a power is that thanks to which we can do something, simply, for example, wax wrathful or trust, but a habit is that thanks to which we do something well or badly, as is said in the *Ethics*. Therefore, where there is a different sense of the good, there is a difference sense of object with respect to habit, but not with respect to power, since there are many habits in one potency.

Ad 5. It should be said that nothing prevents a thing from being the efficient cause of that which is its final cause, as medicine is the efficient cause of health, which is the end of medicine, as the Philosopher says in *Ethics* 1. Therefore, habits are the efficient cause of acts, but acts are the ends of habits, and, therefore, habits are formally distinguished according to their acts.

Ad 6. It should be said that with respect to the end proportioned to human nature, natural inclination suffices in order for a man to be well related to it; that is why the philosophers spoke of various virtues whose object is happiness. But the end in which we hope for happiness, God, exceeds the proportion of our nature, which is why above the natural inclination virtues are necessary which raise us to the ultimate end.

Ad 7. It should be said that to attain God in whatever imperfect way is of greater perfection that to attain other things perfectly. Hence, the Philosopher says in the *Properties of animals* and *On the heavens* 2, that what we grasp of higher things is more worthy than to know much of other things. Therefore, nothing prevents faith and hope from being virtues although by means of them we attain God imperfectly.

Ad 8. It should be said that the affections are ordered to God both through hope, whereby we trust in him, and through charity, whereby we love him.

Ad 9. It should be said that love is the principle and root of all affections, for we do not rejoice in a present good if it is not loved, and the same thing is clear in other affections. Therefore, every virtue which orders some passion also orders love, nor does it follow that charity which is love is not a special virtue, but it must be, as it were, the principle of all the virtues insofar as it moves them all to its end.

Ad 10. It should be said that it is not necessary that all the divine attributes give rise to theological virtues, but only insofar as they move our appetite as an end, and in this respect there are three theological virtues, as was said in article 10 of this question.

Ad 11. It should be said that God is the end of religion, not its object; its object is those things involved in reverencing Him. So it is not a theological virtue. Likewise, the wisdom whereby we contemplate God now does not look immediately to God, but to His effects which are the present means of contemplating him. Moreover, fear looks to something other than God for its object – either punishments or one's insignificance, by thinking of which a man is brought reverently to submit himself to God.

Ad 12. It should be said that just as in speculative matters there are principles and conclusions, so in action there are ends and means. Therefore, for perfect and expeditious knowledge it does not suffice that a man have true knowledge of principles, he also needs knowledge of conclusions. So it is that in action, over and above the theological virtues by which we are well related to the ultimate end, there must be other virtues which order us to the means.

Ad 13. It should be said that, although the good as such is the object of the appetite and not the intellectual part, the good can be found in the intellectual part as well, for to know the true is a kind of good, and thus the habit perfecting intellect in knowledge of the truth has the note of virtue.

Ad 14. It should be said that in its essence prudence is an intellectual virtue, but it has moral matter; therefore, sometimes it is numbered with the moral as existing in a way between intellectual and moral virtues.

Ad 15. It should be said that, although intellectual virtues are distinguished from the moral, they fall to moral science insofar as their acts are subject to will, for we use science when we want to, and likewise with the other intellectual virtues. Something is called moral because it is related in some way to the will.

Ad 16. It should be said that the right reason of prudence is not put in the definition of moral virtue as something of its essence but either as its efficient cause or because of participation, for moral virtue is nothing other than the appetitive part's participation in right reason, as was said in what has gone before.

Ad 17. It should be said that external makeables are the matter of art whereas the matter of prudence are things to be done which are within us. Therefore, just as art requires rectitude in exterior things, which it disposes according to some form, so prudence requires a correct disposition in our passions and affections. For this reason prudence needs moral virtues in the appetitive part, but art does not.

Ad 18. We concede. The appetite of the intellective part, that is, will, bears on a universal good grasped by intellect, but the appetite of the sensitive part does not bear on a universal good anymore than sense can grasp the universal.

Ad 19. It should be said that although appetite is naturally moved by the good as apprehended, in order for it to be inclined easily to the good that reason perfected by prudence grasps, it must have virtue. Particularly when appetite left to itself is drawn to the opposite, it needs true reason deliberating about and showing the good. For example, the is fashioned to be moved by what is delightful to sense and the irascible by revenge, but sometimes, after deliberation, reason forbids these. Likewise the will, with respect to the things that fall to man's use, is so fashioned as to desire what is necessary for its life, but reason after deliberation sometimes commands that it be shared with another. That is why a habit of virtue is needed in the appetitive part in order for it to obey reason with ease.

Ad 20. It should be said that knowledge pertains immediately to prudence, but action pertains to it through the mediation of the appetitive power; therefore, in the appetitive power there must be the habits that are called moral virtues.

Ad 21. It should be said that there is one notion of truth in all moral virtues, for in all there is the true contingent thing to be done, but there is not the same notion of good, which is the object of virtue. Therefore, there is one knowing habit for all moral matters, but not one moral virtue.

Ad 22. It should be said that the mean is found differently in different matter, and ,therefore, the diversity of matter in the moral virtues causes a formal difference insofar as moral virtues differ in species.

Ad 23. It should be said that some special moral virtues with their own special matter appropriate to themselves what is common to all virtues and are denominated from it. Moreover, that which is common to all has a special difficulty and praise in some special matter. For it is clear that every virtue requires that its act be modified according to fitting circumstances by which it is constituted in a mean, and that it be ordered to the end or to something else outside, and again that it have firmness, for to act unchangingly is one of the conditions of virtue, as is clear in *Ethics* 3, and firmly to persist has especial difficulty and praise in mortal danger, and then the virtue bearing on this matter claims for its name fortitude. Restraint in the matter of the pleasures of touch especially involves difficulty and merits praise: the virtue bearing on this is called temperance. In the use of external things rectitude is especially needed and praised in the goods that men share. Therefore, the good of virtue in these is that a man be related to others according to equality, and justice is named from this. Therefore, speaking of virtues, men sometimes use the name of fortitude and temperance and justice, not insofar as they are special virtues with a determinate matter, but with respect to the general conditions from which they are named. That is why it is said that temperance should be brave, that is, have firmness, and fortitude be tempered, that is, to keep to a measure, and so too with the others. It is clear in the case of prudence that it is in some way general, insofar as it has all morals for its matter, and insofar as all moral virtues in a way participate in it, as was shown in this article and in *ad* 16. For this reason every moral virtue ought to be identical with prudence.

Ad 24. It should be said that a virtue is called cardinal, or principal, because other virtues are fixed on it as a door is on its hinges. And since the door is that through which one enters the house, the notion of cardinal virtue does not belong to the theological virtues, which look to the ultimate end from which there is no movement or going into the interior. It does belong to the theological virtues that other virtues are fixed on them as on something unchangeable, which is why faith is called a foundation, 1 Corinthians 3, 11, "For other foundation no one can lay but that which has been laid . . ." and hope an anchor, Hebrews 6, 19, "as a sure and firm anchor of the soul . . . ," charity a root, Ephesians 3, 17, "being rooted and grounded in love . . ." Similarly, the intellectual virtues are not called cardinal because some of them are perfective of the contemplative life, namely, wisdom, science, and understanding, but the contemplative life is the end; hence, it does not have the notion of a door. The active life, which moral virtues perfect, is a door to the contemplative. Although art does not have virtues attached to it that it might be called cardinal, prudence which is directive in the active life is counted among the cardinal virtues.

Ad 25. It should be said that there are two powers of the rational part, namely, the appetitive, which is called will, and the apprehensive, which is called reason. So there are two cardinal virtues in the rational part, prudence with respect to reason and justice with respect to will. In the concupiscible there is temperance and in the irascible fortitude.

Ad 26. It should be said that in any matter there should be a cardinal virtue bearing on that which is principal in that matter. Virtues concerned with other less principal aspects of the matter are called secondary or adjunct virtues. E.g, in concupiscible passions, desires and pleasure, are the chief things with respect to touch, and temperance is concerned with them and is called the cardinal virtue in such matter. But pleasantness (*eutrapelia*), which concerns the pleasures of games, can be posited as a secondary or adjunct virtue. Similarly with the irascible passions: Fear and boldness are the chief things which pertain to mortal peril, and fortitude deals with them, which is why it is called the cardinal virtue in irascible matters, and not meekness, which concerns anger, even though the irascible is denominated from anger: Fortitude concerns that which is ultimate in irascible passions. Magnanimity and humility, which are concerned with hope, and faithfulness is concerned with something greater. Hope and anger do not move a man as does the fear of death With regard to actions concerned with external things useful for life, the first and foremost is that each be accorded what is his own, and this justice does. Absent this, neither liberality nor magnificence can occur, and, therefore, justice is a cardinal virtue and the others adjunct. To command or to choose is the principal act of reason, and this prudence does and to it are ordered *eubulia*, which is deliberative, and then judgment about what has been deliberated, which is the work of *synesis*. That is why prudence is the cardinal virtue and the others adjunct.

Ad 27. It should be said that other adjunct or secondary virtues are listed as integral or subjective parts of the cardinal virtues when they have a matter determined to a proper act, but as potential parts insofar as they participate in a particular way and bear in a lesser way on the mean which belongs principally and more perfectly to the cardinal virtue.

Article 13
Whether virtue lies in a mean

It seems not.

1. As is said in *On the heavens* 1, virtue is the utmost of a power. But the utmost is not a mean, but rather an extreme. Therefore, virtue does not lie in the mean, but in the extreme.

2. Moreover, virtue has the mark of the good, for it is a good quality; Augustine says that the good has the mark of an end, which is the utmost. Therefore, virtue lies in the extreme rather than in the mean.

3. Moreover, good is contrary to evil, and there is no mean between them which would be neither good nor evil, as is said in the Post-Predicaments. Therefore, good has the mark of the extreme, and thus virtue, which makes the one having it good and makes his work good, as is said in *Ethics* 2, lies in the extreme not in the mean.

4. Moreover, virtue is the good of reason, for the virtuous is what is in accord with reason. But reason does not relate to man as a mean but as supreme. Therefore, it is not the note of virtue to lie in the mean.

5. Moreover, every virtue is either theological or intellectual or moral, as is clear from the foregoing. But theological virtue does not lie in the mean: Bernard says that the mode of charity is not to have a mode. But charity is chief among the theological virtues and their root. So too it is not the case that intellectual virtues lie in the mean, because a mean lies between contraries. But things are not contraries as they exist in intellect, nor is intellect destroyed by the excessive intelligible, as is said in *On the soul* 2. So too moral virtues do not seem to lie in the mean, because some virtues consist in the maximum, as bravery is concerned with the greatest peril, which is the peril of death, and magnanimity concerns the highest in honors, and magnificence the greatest in consumables, and piety the greatest reverence, which is owed to parents, to whom we can return nothing equivalent, and the same is true of religion, which is concerned with what is the highest in the divine cult, which we cannot sufficiently serve. Therefore, virtue does lie in the mean.

6. Moreover, if the perfection of virtue consists in the mean, the more perfect virtues would most consist in the mean, but virginity and poverty are more perfect virtues, because they are counsels which deal only with the greater good. Therefore, virginity and poverty are in the mean, which seems false, because virginity abstains from all venereal pleasure, and this is an extreme, and thus it is with poverty with respect to possessions, which rejects them all. Therefore, it is does not seem to be the mark of virtue to lie in the mean.

7. Moreover, Boethius in *On arithmetic* speaks of a threefold mean, the arithmetical, as 6 between 4 and 8, which is an equal distance from both, and the geometrical, as 6 between 9 and 4, which is proportionally the same distance from both, namely, two-thirds, though not the same quantity, and the harmonic or musical mean, as 3 between 6 and 2 because there is the same proportion of one extreme to the other, namely, 3 (which is the difference between 6 and 3) to 1, which is the difference between 2 and 3. But none of these means is found in virtue, since the mean of virtue does not relate equally to extremes, nor in a quantitative way nor according to some proportion of the extremes and differences. Therefore, virtue does not lie in the mean.

8. But it might be replied that virtue consists in the mean of reason, not the real mean of which Boethius speaks. On the contrary, virtue, according to Augustine, is counted among the greatest goods and no one can use them badly. Therefore, if the good of virtue lies in the mean, it would be necessary that the mean of virtue be a mean in the fullest sense of the term. But the real mean has the note of mean more perfectly than does the mean of virtue. Therefore, the mean of virtue would have to be the real mean rather than the mean of reason.

9. Moreover, moral virtue is concerned with the passions and activities of the soul, and they are indivisible. But mean and extremes have no place in the indivisible. Therefore, virtue does not consist in the mean.

10. Moreover, the Philosopher says in the *Topics* that in pleasures present enjoyment is better than past, to be happening than to have happened. But there is a virtue, namely, temperance, that deals with

pleasures. Therefore, since virtue always seeks what is best, temperance always seeks present pleasure, which is to bear on an extreme, not a mean. Therefore moral virtue does not lie in a mean.

11. Moreover, where there is more and less, there is a mean. But in vices there is more and less, since one is more or less carnal or gluttonous. Therefore, in gluttony and lust and in the other vices, there is a mean. Therefore, if it is the note of virtue to lie in the mean, it would seem that virtue must be found in vice.

12. Moreover, if virtue consists of a mean, it can only be the mean between two vices. But this is not true of moral virtue, since justice is not between two vices but has only one opposed vice; to take more than is one's due is vicious, but to take from another what is one's own is not a vice. Therefore, it is not the mark of moral virtue to lie in the mean.

13. Moreover, the mean lies at an equal distance between extremes, but virtue is not equidistant from extremes, since the courageous man is closer to the bold man than to the timid, and the liberal man to the prodigal than to the stingy, and the same is obvious in the others. Therefore, moral virtue does not lie in the mean.

14. Moreover, one goes from extreme to extreme only via the mean. Therefore, if virtue lies in the mean, the only transition from a vice to its opposite would be by way of virtue, which is patently false.

15. Moreover, the mean and the extremes are in the same genus, but courage and timidity and boldness are not in the same genus, since courage is in the genus of virtue and timidity and foolhardiness in the genus of vice. Therefore, courage is not a mean between them. And the same can be said of the other virtues.

16. Moreover, just as the extremes in quantity are indivisible, so is the mean, for the point is both the mean and the term of the line. Therefore, if virtue lies in the mean, it lies in the indivisible. This is also apparent from the Philosopher's statement in *Ethics* 2 that it is difficult to be virtuous, just as it is difficult to hit the target or to find the center of the circle. However, if virtue lies in the indivisible, it seems that virtue neither increases nor decreases, which is manifestly false.

17. Moreover, there is no diversity in the indivisible. Therefore, if virtue lies in the mean as in a kind of indivisible, it seems that there

is no diversity in virtue, such that what is virtuous for one is virtuous for another, which is manifestly false, for something is praised in one and blamed in another.

18. Moreover, whatever is a little bit removed from the indivisible, for example, from the center, is outside the indivisible and outside the center. Therefore, if virtue lies in the mean as in an indivisible, it seems that whatever would fall off a little bit from what it is right to do, would be outside virtue, and thus the man who acts virtuously would be extremely rare. Therefore, virtue does not lie in the mean.

ON THE CONTRARY. A virtue is either moral, intellectual, or theological. But the moral virtue lies in the mean, for moral according the Philosopher in *Ethics* 7 is a habit of choice lying in the mean. Intellectual virtue too seems to lie in the mean, which is why the Apostle says in Romans 12, 3, "Let no one rate himself more than he ought, but let him rate himself according to moderation." So too theological virtue seems to lie in a mean, for faith falls between two heresies, as Boethius says in *On the two natures*; and hope is a mean between presumption and despair. Therefore, every virtue lies in a mean.

RESPONSE. It should be said that moral and intellectual virtues lie in a mean, although differently, but theological virtues do not lie in a mean, except accidentally. In order to see this, one should notice that the good of anything having a rule and a measure lies in its being adequate to its rule or measure; hence, we call that good which has neither more nor less than it should. Notice that human passions and activities are the matter of the moral virtues as things to be done just as things to be made are the matter of art. Therefore, the good in things that come about from art lies in this, that the artifacts are measured by the demands of art, which is the rule of artifacts. So too the good in human passions and activities is to attain the mode of reason, which is the rule and measure of human passions and activities. Since a man is a man because he has reason, his good lies in living in accord with reason. For one to exceed or fall short of the measure of reason in human passions and activities is evil. Therefore, since the human good is human virtue, it follows that moral virtue lies in the mean between too much and too little, insofar as too much, too little, and the mean are read in relation to the rule of reason. Intellectual virtues, which are in reason itself, are either practical, such as prudence and art, or speculative, such as wisdom, science, and understanding. The matter of the practical virtues is human passions and activities or artificial things, whereas the matter of the speculative virtues is necessary things.

Reason relates differently to the two. In those where reason is concerned with works, it is a rule and measure, as has been said. But with respect to the objects of theory, reason is measured and ruled by another rule and measure: The true is our intellect's good and intellect has it when it is adequated to the thing.

Therefore, just as moral virtues consist in a mean determined by reason, the same mean pertains to prudence, which is the practical intellectual virtue concerned with moral matters, insofar as it imposes it on actions and emotions. This is clear from the definition of moral virtue in *Ethics 2*: a choosing habit, consisting in the mean as the wise man would define it. The mean of prudence and of moral virtue is the same, but prudence impresses it, and it is impressed on moral virtue, just as in art reason rules and the artifact is ruled.

In speculative intellectual virtues, the mean is the true itself, which is found in it insofar as it attains its measure. This mean does not lie between contraries as read from the side of things; the contrariety relevant to moral virtue is not that of the measure but of the measured, insofar as it exceeds or falls short of the measure, something clear from what has been said of moral virtues. The contraries between which the mean of intellectual virtues lies is taken from the side of intellect.

The contraries of intellect are opposed on the basis of affirmation and negation, as is clear from *On Interpretation*. The mean of the speculative intellectual virtues, which is the true, is taken from affirmations and their opposed negations. For example, it is true when it is said that what is is and what is not is not. The false involves excess when what is not is said to be and defect when what is is said not to be. If there were no contrariety proper to intellect which differs from the contrariety of things, there would be no mean between extremes in intellectual virtues. It is clear that there is no contrariety proper to will, but only its relation to contrary willed things. The intellect knows something insofar as it is within it whereas will moves toward the thing as it exists in itself. So if there is a virtue in will based on its comparison to a measure and rule, such a virtue would not consist in a mean, for the extremes must be read from the side of the measured alone, not from that of the measure, insofar as it exceeds or falls short of the measure. Theological virtues, however, are ordered to their matter or object, which is God, by the mediation of will, for no one believes unless he is willing. Hence, since God is the rule and measure of the human will, it is manifest that the theological virtues do not lie in a mean, speaking *per se*, although it sometimes happens that some of them lie in a mean accidentally, as will be explained below.

Ad 1. It should be said that the utmost of a power is taken from the utmost to which the power extends, and this is the most difficult, because it is most difficult to find the mean but easy to deviate from it. Thus, virtue is the utmost of a power because it lies in the mean.

Ad 2. It should be said that the good has the note of the ultimate by comparison to the movement of appetite, not by comparison to the matter in which that good is constituted, because it must lie in the mean of the matter, such that it neither exceeds nor is exceeded by the fitting rule and measure.

Ad 3. It should be said that virtue, with respect to the form which it takes from its measure, has the note of an extreme, and thus is opposed to evil as the formed to the unformed, and the commensurate to the incommensurate. But with respect to the matter in which such a measure is impressed, virtue lies in a mean.

Ad 4. It should be said that this argument takes supreme and mean according to the order of the powers of the soul and not according to the matter on which the mode of virtue, that is, the mean, is impressed.

Ad 5. It should be said that there is no mean in theological virtues, as has been said, but there is a mean in intellectual virtues, not between a contrariety in things, but as they are in intellect, according to the contrariety of affirmation and negation, as has been said. But in all moral virtues there is the common note that they lie in a mean. Although some of them attain a maximum, they do so according to the rule of reason, as the brave man faces the greatest peril following reason, namely, when he ought, as he ought, and because he ought. The too much and too little are not read from the quantity of the thing, but by comparison to the rule of reason, as for example it would be too much were one to face dangers when he ought not or for the wrong reason; too little if he does not face them when and how he should.

Ad 6. It should be said that virginity and poverty although they are extremes in reality lie in the mean of reason because the virgin abstains from all venereal pleasure as she ought, namely, for the sake of God, and easily. If she should abstain for the wrong reason, for example, because she finds it hateful as such to have children or to have a spouse, this would be the vice of insensitiveness. But to abstain completely from venereal pleasure for a fitting end is virtuous; those who abstain from such things in order to devote themselves to military matters for the good of the republic are praised for their political virtue.

Ad 7. It should be said that the means spoken of by Boethius lie in things and thus are not relevant to the mean of virtue which is determined by reason. Justice seems to be an exception since it involves both a mean in things and another according to reason: The arithmetical mean is relevant to exchange and the geometrical to distribution, as is clear from *Ethics 5*.

Ad 8. It should be said that mean belongs to virtue not as mean but as the mean of reason, because virtue is the good of man, which is to live according to reason. Hence, it is not necessary that what saves the notion of mean best should pertain to virtue, but what is the mean of reason.

Ad 9. It should be said that the passions and activities of the soul are indivisible as such but divisible incidentally, insofar as more and less are found in them in diverse circumstances. And it is thus that virtue holds the mean in them.

Ad 10. It should be said that in voluptuous matters it is better to be doing than to have done, but 'better' here is not to be understood in terms of the true good, which pertains to virtue, but of the pleasurable good, which pertains to lust. That whose existence lies in its being done no longer exists after it has been done; hence pleasure lies in its occurrence, not in its having occurred.

Ad 11. It should be said that not just any means belongs to virtue, but the mean of reason, and this mean is not found in vices, and there cannot be virtue in vice in the proper sense of the term.

Ad 12. It should be said that justice does not attain the mean in external things when a man takes more for himself, for this disorder of his will is vicious. But that one's property be taken by another is outside his goodness and does not involve the disorder of vice. But the passions of the soul with which the other virtues are concerned are within us; hence their superfluity or falling short amounts to vice in man. Therefore, the other moral virtues are between two vices, but justice is not, because it takes its mean in its proper matter, which pertains *per se* to virtue.

Ad 13. The mean of virtue, it should be said, is the mean of reason and not of things; it is not necessary, therefore, that it be equidistant between extremes, but rather it should be what reason determines. Thus when the good of reason consists chiefly in the restraint of passion, virtue is closer to the less than to the more, as is evident in temperance and patience, but when the good consists in that to which passion leads, virtue is closer to the more, as is clear from courage.

Ad 14. It should be said that, as the Philosopher writes in *Physics 5*, the mean is that which something undergoing continuous change reaches first and the ultimate what it reaches last. Hence it is only in continuous motion that there is passage from one extreme to the other through the mean. But the movement from vice to vice is not a continuous motion and neither are those of will and intellect as they bear on diverse things. So it is not necessary that one move from vice to vice through virtue.

Ad 15. It should be said that even when virtue is in a mean as regards the matter, where the mean is found, still as regards its form — thanks to which it is placed in the genus of the good — it is an extreme, as the Philosopher says in *Ethics 2*.

Ad 16. It should be said that although the mean in which virtue lies is in some way indivisible, still virtue can be more or less intense insofar as a man is more or less disposed to attaining the indivisible, as the bow is pulled more or less in order to hit the indivisible target.

Ad 17. It should be said that the mean of virtue is of reason not of things, as has been mentioned, a mean which lies in the proportion or measuring of things and of emotions to man, and this differs from man to man since something that is a lot for one is a little to another. This is why the virtuous is not the same for everyone.

Ad 18. It should be said that since the mean of virtue is the mean of reason, its indivisibility should be understood with reference to reason. But reason takes as indivisible what has only an imperceptible distance that cannot cause an error, for example, the whole body of the earth is taken as an indivisible point in comparison to the whole heaven. Therefore, the mean of virtue has some latitude.

As for what is said ON THE CONTRARY, it should be conceded with respect to both moral and intellectual virtue, but not theological virtue. For it happens that faith lies between two heresies, but this does not belong to it as such insofar as it is a virtue. And the same should be said of hope, which is between two extremes, not as compared to its own object, but according to the subject's disposition to hope for the supernal.

Disputed Question on the Cardinal Virtues

Article 1
Are prudence, justice, fortitude, and temperance cardinal virtues?

And it seems that they are not.

1. Things which are not distinct ought not to be numbered separately, since distinction is the cause of number, as Damascene says. But the virtues mentioned are not distinguished from one another, for Gregory says in the *Morals on Job* 22: Unless prudence is just and temperate and brave, it is not true prudence, nor is there perfect temperance which is not brave, just, and prudent, nor complete fortitude which is not prudent, temperate, and just, nor true justice which is not prudent, brave, and temperate. Therefore, these should not be called the four cardinal virtues.

2. Moreover, virtues seem to be called cardinal because they are principles of other virtues; hence, what some call cardinal, others call principal, as is clear in Gregory *Morals on Job* 22. But since the end is principal with respect to what is for the sake of the end, the theological virtues which have the ultimate end as their object would seem to have a better claim to be called principal than the virtues mentioned which bear on that which is for the sake of the end. Therefore, the virtues mentioned ought not be called the four cardinal virtues.

3. Moreover, things which belong to different genera ought not be placed in the same ordering. But prudence is in the genus of intellectual virtues, as is clear in *Ethics* 6 and the other three are moral virtues. Therefore, they are unfittingly called the four cardinal virtues.

4. Moreover, among the intellectual virtues wisdom is more prin-

cipal than prudence, as the Philosopher proves in *Ethics* 6, because wisdom is concerned with divine things and prudence with human. Therefore, if any intellectual virtue is to be listed among the cardinal virtues, it should be the more principal one, that is, wisdom.

5. Moreover, other virtues ought to be reduced to the cardinal virtues. But the Philosopher in *Ethics* 2 opposes certain other virtues to fortitude and temperance, namely liberality and magnanimity and the like, which thus are not reduced to them. Therefore, the aforementioned are not cardinal virtues.

6. Moreover, what is not a virtue should not be put among the cardinal virtues. But temperance does not seem to be a virtue, for it is not had when other virtues are had, as is clear in Paul who had all the other virtues yet did not have temperance, for concupiscence remained in his members according to Romans 7, 23: "I see another law in my members, warring against the law of my mind." The temperate man differs from the continent in this, that the temperate man does not have depraved desires, but the continent does, though he does not follow them, as is clear from the Philosopher in *Ethics* 6. Therefore, the foregoing are improperly enumerated as four cardinal virtues.

7. Moreover, just as a man is well-ordered in himself by virtue, so too is he well-ordered to his neighbor. But by two of these virtues a man is ordered to himself, namely, fortitude and temperance. Therefore, there should be two virtues by which he is ordered to his neighbor, and not only justice.

8. Moreover, Augustine says in *On the morals of the church* hat virtue is the order of love. But the love of grace is contained in two precepts, namely, love of God and love of neighbor. Therefore, there should be only two cardinal virtues.

9. Moreover, the diversity of matter due to extension causes only numerical diversity. But the diversity of matter which is due to the reception of different forms causes a generic difference, on account of which the corruptible and incorruptible differ in genus, as is said in *Metaphysics* 10. But the virtues mentioned differ insofar as matter has a different way of receiving form. For the mode of reason in the case of the matter of temperance is to refrain the passions, but in the matter of fortitude to struggle toward that from which passion pulls

away. Therefore, the virtues mentioned differ in genus and ought not to be conjoined in one order of cardinal virtues.

10. Moreover, the definition of virtue is based on the fact that it has to do with reason, as is clear from the Philosopher in *Ethics* 2, who defines virtue as being in accord with right reason. But right reason is a measured measure that is measured by the first measure, God, from whom reason has the power of regulating. Therefore, moral virtues have the note of virtue chiefly insofar as they attain the first measure, God, but the theological virtues, which are concerned with God, are not called cardinal. Therefore, moral virtues ought not be called cardinal.

11. Moreover, reason is the chief part of the soul, but temperance and fortitude are not in reason but in the irrational part, as the Philosopher says in *Ethics 3*. Therefore, they ought not be put among the cardinal virtues.

12. Moreover, it is more laudable to use one's own property than to give or take away another's. But the first pertains to liberality and the second to justice. Therefore, liberality rather than justice ought rather to be called a cardinal virtue.

13. Moreover, that which is the basis of others ought especially to be called a cardinal virtue. But humility is that, for Gregory says that he who has the other virtues without humility carries them as ashes in the wind. Therefore, humility ought to be numbered among the cardinal virtues.

14. Virtue is a kind of perfection, as is clear from the Philosopher in *Physics* 6. But, as is said in James 1, 4, patience has a perfect work. Therefore, as perfection patience ought to be numbered among the cardinal virtues.

15. Moreover, the Philosopher says in *Ethics* 6 that magnanimity does the most among the virtues and is as an ornament to the other virtues. But this especially seems to count toward a virtue's being principal. Therefore, magnanimity seems to be a cardinal virtue and the foregoing are improperly accounted the four cardinal virtues.

ON THE CONTRARY. Ambrose says in commenting on Luke 6, "Blessed are the poor in spirit," that we know there are four cardinal virtues: temperance, justice, prudence, and fortitude.

RESPONSE. It should be said that 'cardinal' comes from the hinge on which a door swings, according to Proverb 26, 14: "As a door turneth upon its hinges, so doth the slothful upon his bed." Hence, cardinal virtues are those on which human life is founded, by which the gate may be entered; but human life is what is proportioned to man.

In man, however, there is found first a sensitive nature, in which he is like the brutes; then practical reason, which is proper to man according to his level; and speculative intellect, which is not found in man as perfectly as it is in the angels, but as a kind of participation on the part of the soul. Therefore, the contemplative life is not properly human but superhuman; the life of pleasure, however, by which one adheres to sensible goods, is not human but bestial.

The properly human life is the active which consists in the exercise of the moral virtues; therefore, those virtues are properly called cardinal on which the moral life somehow turns and is based, as the principles of such a life, which is why these virtues are also called principal.

There are four things involved in the virtuous act. First, that the substance of this act is modified in itself: This is why the act is called good, as bearing on fitting matter or clothed with fitting circumstances. Second, the act must relate fittingly to the subject, that is, be firmly rooted. Third, the act must be fittingly proportioned to something extrinsic to it as an end. These three all follow from the fact that the virtuous act is directed by reason, but a fourth is taken from directing reason, namely, deliberation.

The Philosopher touches on these four in *Ethics 2* when he says that it does not suffice for virtue that things are justly or temperately done, which pertains to the modification of the act. Three other things are required from the side of the agent. First, that he be knowing, which refers to the directing knowledge; then, that he should will and choose for the sake of this: This refers to the rightness of the act as ordered to something extrinsic. Third, that it be stable, such that it firmly and changelessly characterizes the agent and his act. Now these four, namely, directive knowledge, rightness, stability, and moderation, although they are required of every virtuous act, each has a kind of special importance in certain matters and acts.

Three things are required of practical knowledge. The first of which is deliberation, the second is judgment of what has been deliberated; of course, discovery, inquiry and judgment are also found in speculative reason. But because practical reason commands flight or pursuit, something speculative intellect does not do, a point made in *On the Soul 3*, a third note characterizes practical reason, namely, to ponder things which must be done. The other two are ordered to this as to what is principal in practical reason. What Aristotle calls *eubulia* – deliberating well – perfects a man in the first respect, and *synesis* and *gnome* enable a man to judge well, as is said in *Ethics 6*. But it is through prudence that reason is able to command well, as is said in that same place; so it is clear that what is most important in directive knowledge pertains to prudence, and this is why prudence is numbered among the cardinal virtues.

Similarly, the rectitude of the act in comparison to something extrinsic has the note of the good and laudable even in things which pertain to oneself, but is especially praised in the things that pertain to others: that is, when a man makes his act right not only with respect to himself but also with respect to what he has in common with others. For the Philosopher says in *Ethics 5* that many can use virtue in what concerns themselves but cannot in what concerns others; justice is the principal virtue in this regard, since by it a man is adapted and made equal in a fitting way to those with whom he lives. Hence, those things are commonly called just which are adapted in certain way.

Moderation, or restraining, commands praise and has the note of the good chiefly when passion is intense and the restraint of reason is needed if the mean of virtue is to be achieved. Passions are most intense with respect to the greatest pleasures, that is, the pleasures of touch. Temperance is called a cardinal virtue because it restrains the desire for tactile pleasures.

Firmness deserves praise and has the note of the good chiefly when passions induce us to flee, especially in the greatest perils which involve mortal danger. Fortitude is called a cardinal virtue because by it one is intrepid in the face of mortal danger.

Of these four virtues, prudence is in reason, justice in will, fortitude in the irascible, and temperance in the concupiscible, which are the only powers that can be the principles of a human or a voluntary act.

Thus, the meaning of cardinal virtue is clear, both on the side of the modes of virtue, which are its formal notes, and on the side of matter, and on the side of the subject.

Ad 1. It should be said that people speak in two ways of the four cardinal virtues mentioned, for some use these four names to signify general modes of the virtues, for example, calling any directive knowledge prudence, any rectitude that equalizes human acts justice, any moderation that restrains man's appetite for temporal goods temperance, and all firmness of soul stabilizing man in the good against the assault of whatever evils, fortitude. It is in this way that Augustine seems to use these words in *On the morals of the church*, and in this way too that the remark of Gregory can be understood, because only one of the conditions of the true virtue does not suffice: All the conditions must be satisfied. On this basis the four are called virtues not because of different species of habits drawn from diverse objects, but according to different formal notions.

Others however, like Aristotle in the *Ethics*, speak of the four virtues mentioned as special virtues determined to proper matters, and Gregory's remark is true in this sense as well, for by a certain redundancy, these virtues bear on matters in which the four cardinal virtues are most powerfully needed. In this way, fortitude is temperate and temperance brave since one who can restrain his appetite for pleasure, the task of temperance, will more easily restrain the impulse to recklessness before mortal danger; and similarly he who can stand firm against the dangers of death, can all the more easily stand firm against the allurements of desire. On this basis, what belongs principally to temperance passes on to fortitude and vice versa. And the same can be said of the others.

Ad 2. It should be said that man's appetite rests in the end, and, therefore, the principality of the theological virtues, which bear on the ultimate end, is not compared to a hinge, which moves, but rather to a foundation or root, which is standing and at rest, according to Ephesians 3, 17: "rooted and grounded in love."

Ad 3. It should be said that, according to the Philosopher in *Ethics* 6, prudence is right reason with respect to things to be done. But things to be done are called moral works, as is clear from what is said there. Therefore, prudence agrees with the moral virtues because of its matter, and on account of this is numbered among them, although with respect to its essence or subject it is an intellectual virtue.

Ad 4. It should be said that wisdom, because it is concerned with the divine and not the human, does not have its matter in common with the moral virtues, and hence is not numbered among them as if together with them it might be called a cardinal virtue. The notion of hinge is repugnant to contemplation, which is not like a door, whereby one enters into something else, but moral action is the door through which entry is made to the contemplation of wisdom.

Ad 5. It should be said that if the foregoing four virtues are taken to signify the general conditions of virtue, then all the special virtues of which the Philosopher treats in the *Ethics* are reduced to these four as species to genera. But if they be taken as special virtues dealing with the most basic matters, the others are reduced to them as the secondary to the principal; for example, *eutrapelia*, which moderates the pleasure of play, can be reduced to temperance which moderates the pleasures of touch. Hence, Cicero in *Rhetoric* 2 says that the other virtues are parts of these four. That can be understood in two ways: They are subjective parts if these virtues are taken in the first way, whereas they are potential parts if they are taken in the second way. Thus, sense is a potential part of the soul because it does not name the whole power of the soul, but something of it.

Ad 6. It should be said that it is not of the meaning of temperance that it excludes all depraved desires, but that the temperate person does not experience as vehement and strong desires as those who do not try to restrain them. Therefore, Paul suffered inordinate desires because of the corruption of lust, but not strongly or vehemently, because he sought to repress them by castigating his own body and bring it into subjection. Hence, he was truly temperate.

Ad 7. It should be said that justice, by which we are related to the other, does not deal with one's own passions but with the activities by which we communicate with others, such as buying and selling and the like: But temperance and fortitude are concerned with one's own passions and therefore, just as there is one appetitive power without passion, namely, will, and two with passion, namely, the concupiscible and irascible, so there is one cardinal virtue ordered to the neighbor, and two ordering a man to himself.

Ad 8. It should be said that charity is called the whole of virtue not essentially but causally, because charity is the mother of all the virtues. But the effect is always more multiplied than the cause, and therefore the other virtues must be greater in number than charity.

Ad 9. It should be said that the different senses of reception can be taken either from the side of the matter which is receptive of form, and such diversity causes diversity of genus, or from the side of the form which is diversely receivable in matter, and such diversity causes diversity of species. And so it is in the objection.

Ad 10. It should be said that the moral virtues involve reason as their proximate measure, but God as their first measure. Things are specified according to proper and proximate principles, not according to first principles.

Ad 11. It should be said that the rational is the principal part of man, but something is rational in two ways, essentially or by way of participation and, just as reason itself is more principal that the powers participating in reason, so prudence is more principal than the other virtues.

Ad 12. It should be said that the cardinal virtues are called more principal, not because they are more perfect than all the other virtues, but because human life more principally turns on them and the other virtues are based on them. But it is manifest that human life turns more on justice than on liberality, for we use justice in regard to all, but liberality in regard to a few. And liberality itself is founded on justice, for there would not be a liberal gift if one did not give of his own, but one's own is distinguished from that of others through justice.

Ad 13. It should be said that humility strengthens all virtues indirectly by removing what can undermine the good works of the virtues and cause them to perish; but the other virtues are directly strengthened by the cardinal virtues.

Ad 14. It should be said that patience is included in fortitude, for the brave person has what the patient person has, namely, not to be disturbed by imminent evils, but adds even more, namely, that he drives off imminent evils in the way that he should.

Ad 15. It should be said that, from the fact that magnanimity adorns the other virtues, it is clear that it presupposes the other virtues in which it is grounded, and from this it is also clear that the others are more principal than it.

Article 2

Whether the virtues are connected such that he who has one has all

And it seems not.

1. In commenting on Luke, Bede says that the saints are more humbled by the virtues they do not have than extolled for those they have. Therefore, they have some and lack others, and the virtues are not connected.

2. Moreover, a man is in the state of charity after penance, and yet he experiences difficulty in certain matters because of his earlier practice, as Augustine says against Julian. But a difficulty of this kind seems to arise from a habit contrary to virtue, due to an acquired bad inclination incompatible with the contrary virtue. Therefore, someone can have one virtue, namely, charity, and lack others.

3. Moreover, charity is found in all those who have been baptized, but some of the baptized do not have prudence, as is particularly evident in the retarded and insane, who cannot be prudent, according to the Philosopher, and even in some simple adults who do not seem to be prudent, since they do not deliberate well, which is a work of prudence. Therefore, he who has one virtue, namely charity, does not have all the others.

4. Moreover, according to the Philosopher in *Ethics* 6, prudence is right reason concerning things to be done, as art is right reason regarding things to be made. But a man can have right reason with regard to one sort of makeable things, for example, tools, and not with respect to other artificial things. Therefore, he can also have prudence concerning one sort of act, for example, just acts, and not have it concerning another, for example, brave acts. Thus, he will have one virtue without the others.

5. Moreover, the Philosopher says in *Ethics* 6 that not every liberal person is magnificent, yet both liberality and magnificence are virtues; similarly he says that some are moderate and not magnanimous. Therefore, it is not the case that whoever has one virtue has them all.

6. Moreover, the Apostle says in 1 Corinthians 12, 4: "There are varieties of gifts;" and afterwards (8–9) adds: "To one through the

Spirit is given the utterance of wisdom; and to another the utterance of knowledge" (which are intellectual virtues), "to another faith" (which is a theological virtue). Therefore, one can have one virtue and not another.

7. Moreover, virginity is a virtue, as Cyprian says. But many have other virtues and do not have virginity. Therefore, not everyone who has one virtue has them all.

8. Morever, the Philosopher says in *Ethics* 6 that although we call Anaxagoras and Thales wise we do not call them prudent. But wisdom and prudence are intellectual virtues. Therefore, a person can have one virtue without the others.

9. Moreover, in the same book the Philosopher says that some have an inclination to one virtue but not to another. It can happen, therefore, that someone practices the acts of one virtue and not those of another. But from the performance of acts virtues are acquired, as is clear from the Philosopher in *Ethics* 2. Therefore, the acquired virtues at least are not connected.

10. Moreover, although the aptitude for virtue comes from nature it cannot be perfected by nature, as is said in *Ethics* 2. It is manifest as well that it is not from fortune, because the goods of fortune are outside the realm of choice. It follows, therefore, that we acquire virtue either by putting our minds to it or from God. But it seems that one virtue can be acquired intentionally without another since one can have the intention of acquiring one virtue but not another. Similarly, someone can ask God for one virtue and not another. Therefore, in whatever way it be considered, one virtue can be without others.

11. Moreover, in moral matters, the end is related to the acts of the virtues, as principles are to conclusions in demonstrative matters. But a man can have one conclusion without others. Therefore, he can have one virtue without others.

12. Moreover, Augustine says in a letter about the judgment of Jacob that it is not a divine judgment that he who has one virtue has them all, and that a man can have one virtue without the others, for example, mercy and not continence, much as in the body one member can be well, handsome, or healthy, and another not. Therefore, the virtues are not connected.

13. Moreover, things are connected either by reason or principle or subject or object. But the virtues cannot be connected by reason of their principle, God, because then it would follow that all the goods that are from God are connected. Nor by reason of their subject, the soul, because not all are connected on that basis. And not by reason of object, because they are distinguished from one another by their objects and the principle of distinction and connection cannot be the same. Therefore . . .

14. Moreover, the intellectual virtues are not connected with the moral virtues, as is most evident in the understanding of principles, which can be had without the moral virtues. But prudence is an intellectual virtue, which is numbered among the cardinal virtues. Therefore, it does not have a connection with the other cardinal virtues, which are moral virtues.

15. Moreover, in heaven there will be neither faith nor hope, but only charity. Therefore, even in the most perfect state the virtues are not connected.

16. Moreover, angels and separated souls, which are perpetual and immortal, do not have sense powers, and they have charity and justice but not temperance and fortitude because these are virtues of the irrational parts, as is said in *Ethics* 3. Therefore, the virtues are not connected.

17. Moreover, some virtues are of the soul, but there are also virtues of body. But there is no connection among the bodily powers, since one can have sight and not hearing. Therefore, neither is there a connection among the virtues of the soul.

18. Moreover, Gregory says on Ezechiel that no one suddenly becomes the best, and in Psalm 83, 8, it is said: "They shall go from strength to strength." Therefore, a man does not acquire the virtues simultaneously, but successively, and thus the virtues are not connected.

ON THE CONTRARY. 1. Ambrose says in commenting on Luke that they are connected and interlocked such that he who has one is seen to have them all.

2. Moreover, Gregory says in *Morals on Job* 23 that if one virtue could be had without the others, either it is not a virtue or it is not perfect. But perfection is of the very notion of virtue. "For virtue is a certain perfection," as is said in *Physics* 7. Therefore, the virtues are connected.

3. Moreover, with respect to Ezechiel 1, 11: "Two wings of every one were joined," the gloss says the virtues are conjoined such that he who lacks one, lacks the others.

RESPONSE. It should be said that we can speak of virtues in two ways, as perfect and as imperfect. Perfect virtues are connected to one another, but imperfect virtues are not necessarily connected.

In evidence of which it should be noted that since virtue is that which makes a man and his work good, the virtue that makes a man's work and himself good is perfect virtue, whereas the imperfect does not make a man and his work good simply speaking, but only in a certain respect.

Human acts are good simply speaking when they attain to the rule of human acts, one of which is, as it were, homogeneous and proper to man, namely, right reason, and the other a first transcendent measure, which is God. A man attains right reason through prudence, which is right reason concerning what is to be done, as the Philosopher says in *Ethics* 6. A man attains to God through charity, according to John 4, 16: "God is love, and he who abides in love abides in God, and God in him."

There is then a threefold grade of virtue. For there are some wholly imperfect virtues which exist without prudence, not attaining right reason, such as the inclinations which some have to certain works of virtue even from their birth, according to Job 31, 18: "For from my infancy mercy grew up with me: and it came out with me from my mother's womb." Such inclinations are not all at once in everybody, but some have an inclination to one and others to another. Such inclinations do not have the mark of virtue, however, because no one uses a virtue badly, according to Augustine, but a person can use such inclinations badly and harmfully if he acts without discretion, much as a horse if it lacks vision will run faster the harder it is beaten. Hence, Gregory in *Morals on Job* 22 says that other virtues, unless those who desire act prudently, cannot be called virtues at all. Hence, these inclinations without prudence do not fulfill the definition of virtue.

The second grade of virtues are those that attain right reason but do not attain God through charity. These are in a sense perfect with respect to the human good, but not simply speaking perfect, because they do not attain the first rule, which is the ultimate end, as Augustine says against Julianus. Hence, they fall short of the true definition of virtue much as moral inclinations without prudence fall short of the true definition of virtue.

The third grade is of virtues that are perfect simply speaking, because they are with charity. These virtues make a man's act simply good, as attaining the ultimate end. It should be considered further that just as moral virtues cannot exist without prudence, for the reason already given, so prudence cannot exist without the moral virtues, for prudence is right reason about things to be done. For right reason in any genus one must have estimation and judgment of principles, from which reason proceeds, as in geometry one cannot have a correct estimate unless his reason is right concerning geometrical principles. But ends are the principles in things to be done and from them is drawn the reason for acting. But a person has a right estimate of the end thanks to the habit of moral virtue because, as the Philosopher says in *Ethics* 3, as a person is, so does the end appear to him. For to the virtuous that which is the good according to virtue seems desirable as an end, but to the vicious the desirable is that which pertains to his vice. And it is the same with healthy and unhealthy taste. Hence it is necessary that whoever has prudence also has moral virtues.

Similarly, whoever has charity, must have all the other virtues. But charity is in man by a divine infusion, according to Romans 5, 5: "The charity of God is poured forth in our Hearts by the Holy Spirit who has been given to us." But to whomever God gives an inclination he also gives certain forms which are the principles of action and motion to the things God inclines him to, just as he gives lightness to fire so that it can quickly and easily leap upward. Hence, it is said in Wisdom 8, 1: "and ordereth all things sweetly."

So it is necessary that, along with charity, there should be infused habitual forms for expeditiously producing the acts to which charity inclines. But charity inclines to the acts of all the virtues: Since it is concerned with the ultimate end, it implies the acts of all virtues. But any art or virtue which pertains to the end commands those which are for the sake of the end, as the general commands the cavalryman and the cavalryman the maker of harness, as is said in *Ethics* 1. Hence, according to the fittingness of divine wisdom and goodness, along with charity, the habits of all virtues are infused along with charity, and therefore it is said in 1 Corinthians 13, 5: "Charity is patient, is kind," etc.

Therefore, if we mean simply perfect virtues, they are connected because of charity, because no such virtue can be had without charity and, if charity is had, all of them are had. If we understand virtues perfect in the second grade, with respect to the human good, they are connected through prudence, because no moral virtue can be had without prudence nor can prudence be had if one is lacking moral virtue. But if we understand the four cardinal virtues insofar as they imply the general conditions of virtue, in this way they are connected in the sense that it does not suffice to the act of virtue that one of these conditions be present if all are not, and this is the reason Gregory gave for their connection in *Morals on Job* 21.

Ad 1. It should be said that because of an inclination one has to the work of one virtue rather than another, which is either natural or a gift of grace, it happens that one more promptly performs the act of one virtue than another; and in this way the saints are said to have some virtues on which they are prompt to act and not to have others on which they are less prompt to act.

Ad 2. It should be said that although habits as such make someone act promptly and with pleasure, this can be impeded by something supervening, as one having the habit of science is sometimes impeded from using it by sleepiness or drunkenness or something of the like. Therefore, one who repents receives by grace charity and all the other virtues but because of the lingering dispositions from his prior sins he experiences difficulty in the performance of virtues which he has received habitually. This does not happen with virtues acquired through the practice of acts, which at the same time remove contrary dispositions and generate the habits of the virtues.

Ad 3. It should be said that those who are baptized receive prudence along with charity and all the other virtues too, but it is not of the necessity of prudence that a man deliberate well in everything, for example, in trade and military matters and the like, but only in the things necessary for salvation, which are not lacking to those in grace, however simple they be, according to 1 John 2, 27: "But his anointing teaches you concerning all things"; unless perhaps in some of the baptized the act of prudence be impeded on account of the bodily defect of age, as in children or those of deformed dispositions, such as the retarded and mad.

Ad 4. It should be said that artifacts of different types have wholly different principles, so nothing prevents someone having one kind of art and not another. But the principles of morals are so interrelated to one another that the failure of one would entail the failure in others. For example, if one were weak on the principle that concupiscence is not to be followed, which pertains to desire, then sometimes in pursuing concupiscence, he would do injury and thus violate justice. So too in one and the same art or science, for example, geometry, an error about one principle leads to error in the whole science. Thence it is that one cannot be sufficiently prudent with regard to the matter of one virtue unless he is prudent with regard to them all.

Ad 5. It should be said that it happens that someone can be called liberal but not high-minded with respect to an act, because someone having little can use what he has to perform an act of liberality but not of magnificence, although he might have the virtue by which he could also perform the act of magnificence if he had the wherewithal. Similarly, it must be said of moderation and magnanimity. This solution is to be held without reservation in the case of infused virtues, but in virtues acquired through acts it can be said that he who acquired the habit of liberality in the use of little, not yet having acquired the habit of magnificence but actually having the habit of liberality, is in proximate potency to acquiring the habit of magnificence with but slight effort. Therefore, because what is close to being had seems the same as being had, what is lacking only a little seems not to be lacking at all, as is said in *Physics* 2.

Ad 6. It should be said that in those words of the Apostle wisdom and knowledge are understood neither as intellectual virtues, which, however, have no connection, as will be said below, nor as gifts of the Holy Spirit, which are connected through charity, but insofar as they are of grace freely given: namely, insofar as someone abounds in knowledge and wisdom so that he can spur others to the end and to the knowledge of God, convincing those who object. Hence, the Apostle does not say that to one is given wisdom and to another knowledge, but to one is given the utterance of wisdom, to other the utterance of knowledge. Hence, Augustine, in *On the trinity* 14, says that many believers are not strong in such knowledge although they might be strong in faith itself. Faith does not mean here unformed faith, as some say, because the gift of faith is common to all, but means the constancy of faith or its certitude, which sometimes abounds even in sinners.

Ad 7. It should be said that some hold that virginity is not the name of a virtue so much as of a more perfect state of virtue. But it is not necessary that anyone who has a virtue have it in its perfect grade. Therefore, chastity and the other virtues can be had without virginity. Or, if virginity is taken to be a virtue, this will be insofar as it implies a habit of mind by which one chooses to preserve virginity for the sake of Christ. And this habit can exist even in those who are not intact in the flesh, just as the habit of magnificence can be without a lot of wealth.

Ad 8. It should be said that the intellectual virtues are not interconnected and this for three reasons. First, because virtues concerned with different kinds of things are not related to one another, as has been said of the arts. Second, because in the sciences principles and conclusions are not convertible, such that whoever has the principles has the conclusions, as has been said about moral matters. Third, because intellectual virtue is not related to charity by which man is ordered to his ultimate end. Therefore, such virtues are concerned with particular goods, for example, geometry with measuring abstract entities, physics with mobile things, and so on with the others. Hence, they are not connected for the same reason that imperfect virtues are not, as was said about in the body of the article.

Ad 9. It should be said that there are some virtues which order man with respect to the things that occur in human life, such as temperance, justice, patience, and the like, and with them a man must either, while actually performing the act of a virtue, simultaneously perform the acts of the other virtues and thus acquires all habits of the virtues together, or he must be good in the one and bad in the others. But in the latter case, he acquires a habit contrary to a virtue and consequently the corruption of prudence without which, as has been said above in the body of the article, the disposition acquired through the act of any virtue cannot properly be called a virtue. Such acquired habits bearing on things that commonly occur in life are already virtually had as it were in proximate disposition if one has other virtues whose acts frequently occur in human intercourse, as was said of magnificence and magnanimity in the solution of argument 5.

Ad 10. It should be said that acquired virtues are caused purposely, and must be all caused together in a man who proposes to himself to acquire one of them, nor are they acquired unless at the same time one acquires prudence with which all are had, as was said in the body of the article. But infused virtues are caused immediately by God, and they are also caused by charity as by their common root, as was said in the body of the article.

Ad 11. It should be said that in speculative sciences principles and conclusions are not convertible as they are in morals, as was said in the body of the article. Therefore, he who has one conclusion does not necessarily have another. If this were the case, it would be necessary that whoever has the principles has the conclusions, as the objection assumes.

Ad 12. It should be said that Augustine is speaking there of imperfect virtues which are dispositions to the acts of virtues; hence, he himself proves their connection in *On the trinity* 6.

Ad 13. It should be said that virtues are connected by reason of the proximate principle of their genus, which is either prudence or charity, not by reason of the remote and common, which is God.

Ad 14. It should be said that among the intellectual virtues prudence has a special connection with the [moral] virtues by reason of its matter, for it is concerned with changeable things.

Ad 15. It should be said that in heaven where hope and faith disappear certain more perfect things succeed them, namely, vision and comprehension, which are connected with charity.

Ad 16. It should be said that in the angels and separated souls there is not temperance or fortitude with respect to such acts as are performed in this life, namely, moderating the passions of the sensible part, but to other acts, as is evident in Augustine *On the trinity* 14.

Ad 17. It should be said that the powers of the soul are not convertible with its essence, for although no power of the soul can exist apart from essence, yet the essence of the soul can exist without some powers, for example, without sight and hearing because of the corruption of the organs of which such powers are properly the acts.

Ad 18. It should be said that a man is not the best because he has all the virtues but because he has them to the greatest degree.

Article 3

Whether all virtues in a man are equal

And it seems that they are not.

1. For it is said in 1 Corinthians 13,13: "So there abide faith, hope and charity, these three, but the greatest of these is charity." But greatest excludes equality. Therefore, the virtues in a man are not equal.

2. But it will be said that charity is greatest in its act but not as a habit. On the contrary, Augustine says in *On the trinity* that in things that are not quantitatively large, to be greater is the same as to be better. But the habit of charity is better than the habits of the other virtues, because it attains God more, according to 1 John 4, 16, "God abides in him, and he in God." Therefore, charity as a habit is greater than the other virtues.

3. Moreover, perfection precedes the perfectible, but charity is the perfection of the other virtues, according to Colossians 3, 14: "But above all these things have charity, which is the bond of perfection," and in 1 Timothy 1, 5, we read that "the purpose of this charge is charity." Therefore, it is greater than the other virtues.

4. Moreover, that which has nothing of imperfection connected with it is more perfect or greater, because the whiter is that which has no black in it. But the habit of charity has no imperfection mixed with it, because faith is of things unseen and hope of what is not had. Therefore, charity, even as a habit, is more perfect and greater than faith and hope.

5. Moreover, Augustine, in *The City of God* 19 says that, unless virtues are referred to God, they are vices. From which can be gathered that the notion of virtue is perfected by an ordering to God. But charity more proximately orders man to God than the other virtues, because it unites man to God, according to 1 Corinthians 6, 17: "But he who cleaves to the Lord is one spirit with him." Therefore, charity is a greater virtue than the others.

6. Moreover, the infused virtues have their origin in grace which is their perfection. But charity participates in grace more perfectly than the other virtues do, because charity and grace inseparably accompany one another, but faith and hope can be without grace.

Therefore, since charity is greater than the other virtues, not all virtues are equal.

7. Moreover, Bernard says in *On consideration* 1 that prudence is the matter of fortitude, because without prudence fortitude is precipitous. But that which is the principle and cause of something is greater and more powerful than it. Therefore prudence is greater than fortitude. Therefore, not all virtues are equal.

8. Moreover, the Philosopher in *Ethics* 5 says that justice is the whole of virtue, and the other virtues are by way of being parts. But the whole is greater than its part. Therefore, justice is greater than the other virtues, so not all virtues are equal.

9. Moreover, Augustine, in his *Literal commentary on Genesis* 6, says that if everything in the universe were equal, not all of them would exist. But the virtues are all had at once because they are connected, as the preceding article showed. Therefore, not all virtues are equal.

10. Moreover, the vices are opposed to the virtues, but not all vices are equal. Therefore, neither are the virtues equal.

11. Moreover, the acts of virtue ought to be praised, but some people are more praised for one virtue than for another. Hence, Cassian says in *On the Cenobitic constitution* 5: One is adorned with the flowers of knowledge; another by reason of an uncommonly robust discretion; another is founded on the gravity of patience; another of humility; another is preferred for the virtue of continence. Therefore, not all the virtues in a man are equal.

12. But it will be said that this is an inequality on the side of acts, not of habits. On the contrary, according to the Philosopher in *Posterior Analytics* 1, things which are for the sake of something are intended at the same time as the end. But habit by definition is related to act. For habit is that by which one acts when the time is ripe, as Augustine says in *On the conjugal good*. Therefore, if the act of one virtue in a man is greater than the act of another, it follows that the habits too are unequal.

13. Moreover, Hugh of St. Victor says that acts augment habits. Therefore, if the acts of virtues are unequal, their habits too will be unequal.

14. Moreover, in morals the habit of virtue relates to its proper act just as in natural things form relates to its proper motion or ac-

tion. But the more of form a natural thing has, the more it has of activity or motion; for example what is heavier falls more swiftly, and what is warmer heats better. Therefore, in morals too the acts of virtues can only be unequal if the habits of the virtues are unequal.

15. Moreover, perfections are proportionate to the things perfected. But virtues are perfections of powers of the soul which are unequal, since reason excels the lower powers which it commands. Therefore, the virtues are unequal.

16. Moreover, Gregory in *Morals on Job* 22 and in his fifteenth homily on Ezechiel says that blessed Job, because he saw how differently the highest gift was distributed among men, called the increments of virtues steps, since by them they rise and come to attain celestial things. But where there is increment and grades there is no equality. Therefore, the virtues are not equal.

17. Moreover, things so related that the increase of one causes the decrease of another must be unequal. But when charity increases something else seems to decrease, because the condition of heaven, where charity is perfected, is opposed to the condition of the wayfarer where faith plays a role. When one of opposites increases the other decreases. Therefore charity and faith cannot be equal, so not all virtues are equal.

ON THE CONTRARY. 1. Apocalypse 21, 16, says: "And the city stands foursquare, and its length is as great as its breadth." The virtues are meant by the walls of the city, according to the gloss. Therefore the virtues are equal.

2. Moreover, as Augustine says in *On the trinity* 6, 4: "Those who are equal in fortitude are equal in prudence and temperance. For if you should say that some are equal in fortitude but prudence is greater than fortitude, it follows that the fortitude of one is less prudent. And then they will not be equal in fortitude since this one's fortitude is more prudent. And you will find the same in the other virtues, if you apply the same consideration to all." Thus, those who are equal in one virtue need not be equal in others, unless all virtues in the same man are equal.

3. Moreover, Gregory says in commenting on Ezechiel that

faith, hope, charity, and action are equal. Therefore, by parity of reasoning, the other virtues are equal.

4. Moreover, Ezechiel 46, 22, says that there are four measures of one thing, that is, of the way we advance to virtue, according to the gloss. But things that have the same measure are equal. Therefore, all are equal.

5. Moreover, Damascene says that virtues are natural, and are equally in everyone in the mode of being of accident. Therefore, virtues insofar as they are accidents are equal.

6. Moreover, the greater the virtue, the greater the reward. Therefore, if in man there were one virtue greater than another, it would follow that the same man is owed greater and lesser praise, which is absurd.

7. Moreover, if simply follows on simply, then more follows on more. But when one virtue is had, all are had, because the virtues are connected, as was said above in the preceding article. Therefore, if one virtue were had more, it would follow that all were had more. Therefore, it is necessary that all virtues are equal.

RESPONSE. It should be said that things are called equal or unequal with reference to quantity. For things one in quantity are called equal, things one in quality, similar, and things one in substance, the same, as is clear from *Metaphysics* 5. But quantity implies the note of measure, which is found first in numbers, secondarily in magnitudes, and in a different manner in the other genera, as is clear from *Metaphysics* 9.

For in every genus that which is most simple and perfect is the measure of all else, as whiteness in colors and diurnal motion in movements, because a thing is more perfect to the degree that it approaches the first principle of its genus. From this it is evident that insofar as a thing's perfection pertains to its measurement it is from the first principle; and so too its quantity; and this is what Augustine says in *On the trinity* 8 that in things which are not great in quantity, the better and the greater are the same. But since the existence of any non-subsistent form consists in its being in a subject or matter, the perfection of its quantity is of two kinds: one, according to the proper notion of the species; another, according to the existence it has in the matter or subject.

With respect to the proper notion of species, the forms of different species are unequal, but in the same species some forms can indeed be equals and some not. The specific principle must be taken from something indivisible. For the difference in such a principle causes the species to vary and therefore by the addition or subtraction of this principle the species necessarily vary. Hence, the Philosopher says in *Metaphysics* 8 that the species of things are like numbers, in which a unit added or taken away changes the species.

There are some forms that are specified by something of their essence, such as all absolute forms, whether substantial or accidental, and in such it is impossible that in this mode one form be greater than another of the same species, for there is not one whiteness which, considered in itself, could be greater than another. But other forms are specified by something extrinsic to which they are ordered, as motion is specified by its term. Hence, one motion is greater than another as it is closer to or more distant from the term. Similarly, there are some qualities which are dispositions related to something, as health is a certain commensuration of humors ordered to the nature of the animal. Therefore, what is called healthy in a lion would be illness in a man.

Health is not specified by the degree of commensuration but by the nature of the animal to which it is ordered, and it also happens that the same animal is at some times healthier than at others, as is said in *Ethics* 10, insofar, that is, as there can be different degrees of commensuration of humors which realize what is fitting to human nature. And the same is true of science which derives its unity from the unity of the subject, so that geometry can be greater in one person than another insofar as the former knows more conclusions conveying knowledge of the subject of geometry, which is extension.

Similarly too according to the quantity of perfection such forms have insofar as they are in a matter or subject, forms of the same species can be unequal insofar as they inhere more or less, because, as has been said, the specific principle should consist in something indivisible. That is why no substantial form is more or less.

Similarly, if a form is specified by something indivisible in its notion, it will not admit of more or less. No more does two or any other species of number specified by the addition of a unit admit of more and less; nor do figures which are specified by number, like triangle and quadrilateral; nor determined quantities like the cube and pyramid; nor finally numerical relations, such as double and triple.

But forms which neither give species to their subject nor take their species from something indivisible in its notion, can inhere more or less; e.g., whiteness and blackness and the like.

From all this it is evident that there are two ways in which equality and inequality pertain to forms.

Forms specifically the same are unequal neither in themselves, as if one form could be greater than another of the same species, nor according to existence, such that it inheres more in the subject. This is the case with all substantial forms. Other forms do not admit inequality as such but only insofar as they are in a subject, like whiteness and blackness.

Some forms admit inequality in themselves but not as they exist in a subject; for example, one triangle is greater than another, because the base of one is larger than that the other, although they are specified in the same way so the one surface is not more of a triangle than another.

There are some forms that admit inequality both in themselves and insofar as they exist in a subject, for example, health, knowledge, motion. Motions are unequal either because they cover more or less space, or because the moved moves more swiftly. Similarly too one person's knowledge is greater than another's either because he knows more conclusions or because he knows the same things better. So too health can be unequal either because the level of commensuration in one is closer to fitting and perfect equality than in another, and better.

Speaking of the equality and inequality of virtues against this background, we can say that, considered in themselves, specifically different virtues can be unequal. For since virtue is a disposition of the perfect to the best, as is said in *Ethics* 7, that virtue is more perfect and greater which is ordered to the greater good. Given this, the theological virtues, whose object is God, are stronger than the others, and among them charity is the greatest because it unites us more closely to God, and hope is greater than faith, because hope moves the will to God, whereas by faith God is in a man by way of knowledge.

Among all the other virtues prudence is the greatest because it governs the others, and after it comes justice by which a man is well ordered not only in himself but also with respect to others. After this comes fortitude by which a man disregards the perils of death for the sake of the good. Then comes temperance which disregards the greatest of bodily pleasures.

But the kind of inequality found in science cannot be found within a species of virtue. Although it is not of the definition of science that anyone having the science should know all its conclusions, it is of the definition of virtue that one having it is well ordered with respect to everything pertaining to that virtue.

As to the perfection or quantity of virtue insofar as it exists in a subject, there can be inequality even in the same species of virtue when one of those having the virtue is better related than others to the things pertaining to that virtue; and this because of a better natural disposition, or greater exercise, or a better judgment of reason, or a gift of grace. Virtue does not give species to its subject, nor does it have anything indivisible in its notion, *pace* the Stoics who taught that no one has a virtue unless he has it to the maximum, so everyone would have the same virtue equally.

But this does not seem to be the meaning of any virtue, because diversity in the manner of participating in the virtue is gauged by the factors just mentioned, which do not enter into the definition of any particular virtue, for example, chastity and the like.

Therefore, virtues can be unequal in different people, not only with respect to specifically different virtues but also to virtues specifically the same according as they exist in the subject.

But in one and the same man virtues are unequal according to the quantity or perfection a virtue has of itself; but according to the virtue's quantity and perfection as existing in a subject, all virtues must, simply speaking, be equal for the same reason that they are connected, since equality is a kind of connection in quantity. Hence, some give as the reason for equality that the four cardinal virtues are understood as general modes of virtue, and this is the reason of Augustine in *On the trinity* 6. It can be otherwise assigned according to the dependence of moral virtues on prudence and of all virtues on charity. Hence, where charity is equal, all virtues must be equal according to the formal perfection of virtue, and for the same reason prudence with respect to the moral virtues.

In a certain respect, however, virtues in one and the same person can be called unequal and not connected because of the power's inclination to act, which is from nature or some other cause. Because of this some call them unequal in act, but this must be understood only as an inequality of inclination to act.

Ad 1. This argument, it should be said, is based on the inequality of the virtues themselves, not of the inequality in the way they inhere, of which we are now speaking. For charity, as has been said, taken as such, is greater than all other virtues, and yet, as it grows in a person, all the other virtues grow proportionately, as the fingers of the hand are unequal to one another, yet grow proportionately.

Ad 2–7. Similarly, it should be replied to the second, third, fourth, fifth, and sixth, and the seventh too, which in the same fashion argued that fortitude was greater than the other virtues.

Ad 8. Similarly to the eighth, which proceeds in the same way concerning justice; although justice is the whole of virtue, it is not justice in that sense that is called a cardinal virtue.

Ad 9. And we should answer the ninth objection in the same way, because it is insofar as the virtues are in man that greater or less perfection of a species of virtue is distinguished.

Ad 10. Similarly it should be replied to the tenth, because in this way the vices too are unequal.

Ad 11. It should be said that a person is more praised for one virtue than for another because of a greater promptitude to act.

Ad 12. It should be said that where there is a greater habit there should be a greater act according to the inclination of the habit. But there can be something in a man that either impedes action or disposes to it yet is incidentally related to the habit, as one might be impeded from exercising the habit of science because of drunkenness. Therefore, with respect to such impediments or aids to action there can sometimes be an increase in the act without an increase in the habit.

Ad 13. It should be said that in acquired habits greater exercise causes a greater habit; however, a habit acquired through many acts can still be incidentally impeded and not produce its act, as was said in the body of the article.

Ad 14. It should be said that in natural things where there is equal form there can be inequality of act due to some incidental impediment.

Ad 15. It should be said that powers are unequal in themselves, insofar as one power is more perfect than another according to its proper definition. And it has been said that virtues are unequal in this way too.

Ad 16. It should be said that virtues inhere proportionately, as has been said; hence, the condition of heaven is opposed to faith by reason of open vision which one does not attain through an increase of charity; so it does not follow that faith decreases as charity increases.

Responses to arguments advanced On the Contrary:

Ad 1–4. The answers are evident from what has been said.

Ad 5. It should be said that Damascene understands the virtues to be equally in all.

Ad 6. It should be said that the essential reward responds to the root of charity; therefore, even if it be granted that the virtues are not equal, still the same reward is owed to a given man because of the identity of charity.

Ad 7. We concede this point.

Article 4
Whether all the cardinal virtues remain in heaven

And it seems that they do not.

1. For Gregory says in *Morals on Job* 16 that the accidents disposed for life pass away with the body. Therefore, they do not remain in heaven.

2. Moreover, once the end is attained, that which was for the sake of the end is no longer necessary: When one has come to port the ship is no longer necessary. But the cardinal virtues are distinct from the theological virtues in this, that the theological virtues have the ultimate end for their object whereas the cardinal virtues are concerned with what is for the sake of the end. Therefore, when the ultimate end has been attained in heaven, the cardinal virtues will no longer be necessary.

3. Moreover, take away the end and that which is for the sake of the end ceases. But the cardinal virtues are ordered to the civil good, which is not in heaven. Therefore, the cardinal virtues will not remain in heaven.

4. Moreover, that which does not remain according to its proper species but only according to some common notion of the genus is said not to remain in heaven, as faith is said to disappear although knowledge, which is its genus, remains. But cardinal virtues do not remain in heaven according to their distinct proper species, for Augustine says in the *Literal commentary on Genesis* 12 that the one and complete virtue there is to love what you see. Therefore, the cardinal virtues do not remain in heaven, but pass away.

5. Moreover, virtues are specified by their objects. But the objects of the cardinal virtues do not remain in heaven, for prudence is concerned with the doubtful matters on which counsel is taken, justice with contracts and judgments, fortitude with deadly perils, and temperance with desires for food and sex, none of which obtain in heaven.

6. It might be said that in heaven they will have other acts. On the contrary, the difference of a thing, which enters into its definition, specifies it, but act enters into the definition of habit, for Augustine says, in *On the conjugal good*, that a habit is that thanks to which one

acts when the time is propitious. Therefore, if their acts are different, the habits will be specifically different.

7. Moreover, according to Plotinus, as reported by Macrobius, the virtues of the purged soul differ from political virtues. But the virtues of the purged soul would seem especially to be found in heaven, while the virtues of here below are the political virtues. Therefore virtues of this life will not remain but disappear.

8. Moreover, the condition of the blessed differs from that of wayfarers more than do those of master and slave or of husband and wife in the present life. But, according to the Philosopher in *Politics* 1, the virtues of the master differ from the virtues of the servant, and similarly the husband's from the wife's. Therefore, the virtues of wayfarers and of those in heaven must differ even more.

9. Moreover, virtuous habits are needed to facilitate the possibility of acting. But this comes about sufficiently through glory. Therefore, virtuous habits are not necessary.

10. Moreover, in 1 Corinthians 13, 8, the Apostle proves that charity is more excellent than the others because it does not pass away. But faith and hope, which pass away, are more noble than the cardinal virtues because they have a more noble object, namely, God. Therefore, the cardinal virtues pass away.

11. Moreover, the intellectual virtues are more noble than the moral, as is evident in *Ethics* 6. But the intellectual virtues do not remain, because science is destroyed, as is said in 1 Corinthians 13, 8. Therefore, the cardinal virtues will not remain in heaven.

12. Moreover, as is said in James 1, 4, "And let patience have its perfect work." But patience remains in heaven only as a reward, as Augustine says in *On the city of God* 14. Much less then will the cardinal virtues remain.

13. Moreover, some cardinal virtues, namely temperance and fortitude, are in the sense powers of the soul, for, as the Philosopher says in *Ethics* 3, they are of the irrational parts of the soul, as is evident from what the Philosopher says in *Ethics* 3. But the sense parts of soul are neither in angels nor in the separated soul. Therefore, such virtues are not in heaven, neither in the angels nor in the separated souls.

14. Moreover, Augustine says in *On the city of God* 13 that in

heaven we will have leisure, will see, will love and praise. But to have leisure is an act of wisdom, seeing of intellect, loving of charity, praising of worship. Therefore, only these remain in heaven and not the cardinal virtues.

15. Moreover, in heaven men will be like angels, as is said in Matthew 22, 30, but men do not become like angels by sobriety, since they do not use food and drink. Therefore, sobriety will not be in heaven, and by parity of reasoning no other such virtues.

ON THE CONTRARY. 1. There is what is said in Wisdom 1, 15: "For justice is perpetual and immortal."

2. Moreover, Wisdom 7, 7, says, "Wherefore I wished, and understanding was given me: and I called upon God, and the spirit of wisdom came upon me." But nothing is more useful for men in this life, and in heaven there will be the fullest participation in wisdom. Therefore, such virtues will be more fully had in heaven.

3. Moreover, virtues are spiritual riches. But there is a greater treasury of spiritual riches in heaven than in this life. Therefore, such virtues abound in heaven.

RESPONSE. It should he said that the cardinal virtues remain in heaven and will there have other acts than here, as Augustine says in *On the trinity* 13, 8 & 9: "What justice now does in succoring the miserable, what prudence does in forestalling harm, what fortitude in resisting evils, what temperance in restraining depraved pleasures, will not be there where there is no evil at all, but by justice one will be subject to the ruling God, by prudence one will neither prefer nor equate any other good to God, by fortitude adhere to him most firmly, by temperance taking delight in no harmful desire."

In evidence of which it should be known that, as the Philosopher says in *On the heavens* 1, virtue implies the ultimate of a power. Obviously there is a different ultimate in power in different natures, since higher natures have higher powers extending to more and greater things. Therefore, what is a virtue in one is not a virtue in another. For example, virtue in man bears on the most important things in human life; human temperance lies in not departing from reason because of great pleasures, but rather moderating them according to reason; human fortitude consists of standing firm against the greatest perils, deadly perils, for the sake of the good of reason.

But the ultimate of divine power is not in terms of these but of something higher pertaining to the infinity of his power. Therefore, divine fortitude is his changelessness; temperance, the turning of the divine mind on itself; prudence is the divine mind itself; and the justice of God is his perennial law.

It must be noticed that the difference in ultimates can be understood in two ways. First, when they are in the same series of motion; second, when they are wholly disparate, and not ordered to one another. If different ultimates are understood in the first sense, they will cause different species of motion, but they will not diversify the species of the first motor because the same principle of motion moves from beginning to end. Take the example from building where the ultimate term is the completed form of the house; but other ultimates occur as different parts of the house are completed. Hence, as the Philosopher says in *Ethics* 10, one kind of movement terminates in the foundation of the house, another in the superstructure, and another in the complete edifice, yet the building art is one and the same and is the principle of these three changes. And it is the same with other movements.

But if we understand different ultimates, not in a continuous change, but wholly disparate, then both the changes and the moving principles are specifically different. For example, the art of building a house is different from the art of building a ship.

Therefore, where the ultimate is specifically the same, there is the same species of virtue, and the same act or movement of the virtue. Clearly, the ultimate that temperance achieves in me and in you is specifically the same, namely, the moderating of the pleasures of touch. Hence, neither temperance nor its act is specifically different in me and in you. But where the ultimate that a virtue attains is neither specifically the same nor in the same series of movement, there must be a specific difference not only in the act of the virtue but also in the virtue itself. This is clear insofar as these virtues are said to be from God and from man. But where the ultimate of a virtue is specifically different (yet it is contained in the same series of movements, so that by the one another is achieved), the acts are specifically different but the virtue is the same. For example, the act of fortitude aims at one ultimate before the battle and another during battle and at yet another in victory: It is one kind of act to go to war, another to stand bravely in battle, and yet another to rejoice in the victory achieved. But it is the same fortitude, just as to love, desire, and rejoice are acts of the same power.

It is clear from what has been said in this article that, since our state in heaven is higher than our state in this life, the former attains something that is more perfectly the utmost. If then the utmost attained by virtues in this life is ordered to the utmost attained by the virtues in heaven, they must be specifically the same virtues, although their acts will be different. If they are not taken as ordered one to the other, then they will not be the same virtues nor the same act nor the same habit.

But it is obvious that the acquired virtues, of which the philosophers spoke, are ordered only to perfecting men in civil life, not as they are ordered to achieving celestial glory. Therefore, they taught that such virtues do not remain after this life, as Augustine reports of Cicero.

But the cardinal virtues, insofar as they are gratuitous and infused, as we speak of them now, perfect man in the present life as ordered to celestial glory. Therefore, we must say that the habit of these virtues is the same here and there, but that the acts differ, for here they have acts appropriate to those striving for the ultimate end, but there they have acts which are appropriate to those who are already at rest in the ultimate end.

Ad 1. It should be said that such virtues perfect man in the active life, as on a kind of path leading to the term of contemplation in heaven; and they remain in heaven in the acts consummated by the end.

Ad 2. It should be said that the cardinal virtues deal with what is for the sake of the end, not as if these might be their ultimate term, as the ultimate term of the ship is navigation, but insofar as they are ordered to the ultimate end by way of the things that are for the sake of the end. The temperance infused by grace does not have for its ultimate end the moderation of the pleasures of touch, but does this for the sake of celestial similitude.

Ad 3. It should be said that the civil good is not the ultimate end of the infused cardinal virtues, of which we speak, but of the acquired virtues of which philosophers spoke, as was said in the body of the article.

Ad 4. It should be said that nothing prevents one and the same thing from being the end of different virtues or arts. The preservation of the civil good is the end and term of both the army and of positive law; hence both arts and virtues have acts concerned with it as a final good, but the military provides for the preservation of the civil good insofar as brave battles bring it about, whereas positive law rejoices in the same end insofar as the civil good is preserved by the ordinances of law. Therefore, the enjoyment of God in heaven is the end of all the cardinal virtues, and there each rejoices in it, insofar as it is the end of his acts. That is why it is said that in heaven there will be one virtue, inasmuch as one subject will have that in which all the virtues rejoice; however, there will be different acts and different virtues according to the different reasons for rejoicing.

Ad 5. It should be said that something is called the object of a virtue in two ways. In one way, as that to which the virtue is ordered as to its end, as the highest good is the object of charity and eternal happiness the object of hope. In another way, as the matter on which it acts, as tending from it to another, and in this way the pleasures of coition are the object of temperance, for temperance does not intend attachment to such pleasures but intends the good of reason by constraining them. Similarly, fortitude does not intend to dwell on perils but by overcoming them to attain the good of reason, and the same is the case with reason with respect to doubts, and of justice in respect to the necessities of this life. Therefore, the greater the distance from these as the spiritual life develops, the more perfect the acts of these virtues, because the foregoing words refer to these virtues by way of a term *from which* rather than of a term *toward which*, which specifies the act.

Ad 6. It should be said that not every difference in acts points to a diversity of habits, as has already been said in the body of the article.

Ad 7. It should be said that the virtues of the purged soul that Plotinus defined can belong to the blessed, for there prudence only intuits the divine, temperance forgets desire, fortitude ignores the passions, and justice consists in a perpetual covenant with God. But the political virtues of which he speaks are ordered only to the civil good of the present life, as was said in the body of the article.

Ad 8. It should be said that the ultimate of the virtues of master and servant and of husband and wife are ordered to one another, such that from one there can be a transition to the other, so the case is not similar.

Ad 9. It should be said that facilitation of the works of the virtues, that comes about or is perfected by glory, pertains to these habits of virtue.

Ad 10. It should be said that faith is ordered to a truth that is not seen and hope to something arduous not yet had, and these specify them. Therefore, although they are more excellent than the cardinal virtues with respect to their higher object, nonetheless they pass away because they are specified by what does not remain.

Ad 11. It should be said that knowledge is not destroyed as a habit but it has another act.

Ad 12. It should be said that patience does not remain in heaven according to the act that it has in this life, namely, tolerating tribulations, but remains according to an act appropriate to the end, as was said of the other virtues in the body of the article.

Ad 13. It should be said that some teach that the irascible and concupiscible, the subjects of temperance and fortitude, are in the higher part, not in the sensitive part of the soul. But this conflicts with what the Philosopher says in *Ethics* 3, namely, that virtues are in the irrational parts.

Others say that the powers of the sensitive part remain in the separated soul either according to potency alone or according to act. But this cannot be because the acts of the sensitive power cannot exist without the body; otherwise the sensitive soul of the brutes would be incorruptible, which is erroneous.

The object of the act is the object of the power; hence, such powers are connected; and thus after death they do not remain in the actually separated soul, save virtually, as in a root because the powers of the soul flow from its essence. But these virtues are in the irascible so far as their derivation goes, but according to origin and beginning they are in reason and will, because choice is the principle act of moral virtue and it is an act of rational appetite. But by a kind of application this choice terminates in the passions of the irascible and concupiscible because of temperance and fortitude.

Ad 14. It should be said that all four of these pertain to each act of the cardinal virtues in the manner of end, insofar as celestial happiness consists of them.

Ad 15. It should be said that sobriety does not make us like the angels according to the act of this life which bears on the matter of food and drink, but according to the act of heaven where it bears on the ultimate end, like the other virtues.